PLANNING A PERFECT
LIVING ROOM

CREATIVE HOMEOWNER PRESS®

CONTENTS

Based on *Creating a Home,*
First Edition © Eaglemoss Publications Limited 1986, 1987, 1988

Printed at Webcrafters, Inc.,
Madison, Wisconsin, U.S.A.

Current printing (last digit)
10 9 8 7 6 5 4 3 2

Creative Director: Warren Ramezzana
Editor: Kimberly Kerrigone
Copy Editor: Carolyn Anderson-Feighner
Cover Photograph: Syndication International
Design Consultant: Eve Ardia, ASID, Saddle River Interiors

Library of Congress Catalog Number: 91-071691
ISBN 0-932944-95-7 (paper)

CREATIVE HOMEOWNER PRESS® BOOK SERIES
A DIVISION OF FEDERAL MARKETING CORP.
24 PARK WAY
UPPER SADDLE RIVER, NJ 07458-2311

INTRODUCTION

The living room is one of the most important rooms in your home to plan and design. A well thought out living area is the focal point – and the showcase – of the entire house.

In the past, most houses kept a separate room for special occasions and entertaining guests. The family lived in the kitchen and even ate there if they did not have a separate dining room. Today, however, living rooms work harder than in the past to satisfy numerous functions. You may want to relax there after a hard day or entertain guests in an uncluttered, welcoming atmosphere. But this competes with the family's demands for somewhere to watch television, listen to music, study, play and snack. It is these conflicting demands that make designing the living room a challenge.

Planning a Perfect Living Room shows how to accommodate all the functions of this room without sacrificing style and comfort – whether you plan to knock down walls to increase the size of the living area or simply rearrange the furniture to make better use of the space.

Straightforward instructions and clear line drawings show how to draw up the type of plans used by professional interior designers – the essential groundwork of any well-designed room.

Planning a Perfect Living Room contains chapters that review seating, occasional furniture and storage units to guide you through the bewildering range of styles of living room furniture available today. And, vital for creating the right ambience in a room as well as for specific tasks, lighting gets special attention.

Throughout this book there are practical suggestions and lavish color photographs to help inspire you to create the perfect living room.

MEASURE THE LIVING ROOM

Knowing the measurements of a room helps you estimate quantities and plan the layout accurately and easily.

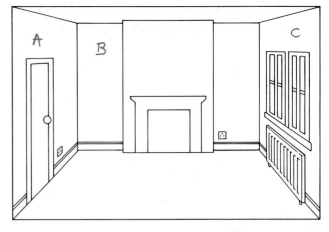

Plans of floors and walls are invaluable when you start to design a room from scratch or wish to give a new look to a room by rearranging the furniture.

☐ When you are redecorating, plans are essential to estimate quantities of materials accurately.

☐ If you are moving, a floor plan for each room in your new home will help you work out what will fit where and also show the furniture movers exactly where to position the pieces.

☐ If you are making any alterations to your home, you can work out ideas to discuss with an architect, and produce plans to show your builder, plumber or electrician exactly what you want.

FEET OR METERS?

Some manufacturers work in metric measurements especially if their goods are imported from overseas.

If you are measuring for something specific – such as an alcove cupboard, floor tiles or wallcovering – find out which system the manufacturer of your chosen product uses.

Avoid measuring in one system, then converting to another. Conversions can not always be precise, for example, a yard is less than a meter (one meter equals approximately 3.28 feet or 39.37 inches). If something needs to fit exactly, being a few centimeters – even millimeters – off can be disastrous.

DRAWING A FLOOR PLAN

The sketch (top right) shows a typical room in an older house or apartment, but measuring is the same for any room. (The letters A, B and C indicate the walls in the floor plan below.)

Making a rough sketch Start by making a rough outline sketch of the room on which to jot down your measurements. Don't worry if it looks out of proportion.

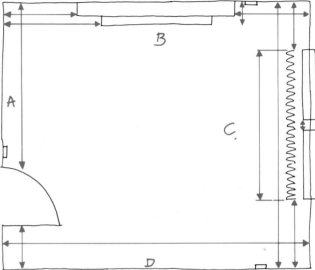

Top: view of room. Above: rough sketch of floor plan.

Mark the position of doors, windows, radiators, electrical outlets, light switches, fireplaces and other permanent features on the rough sketch. Show which way the doors open, and also the windows if they swivel or pivot.

It is customary to mark in windows, radiators, switches, and so on, on floor plans even if they are not at floor level.

Filling in the measurements It's much easier to measure if you have a helper. Work around the room systematically; start at one corner and run the tape along the floor, keeping it straight and parallel to the wall you are measuring (if the tape is angled, the measurements will be inaccurate). As you take each measurement, mark it on the sketch.

If there is a feature jutting out from the wall, run the tape from wall to wall in front of the feature, and then mark on your plan the measurements:

☐ from first wall to fireplace
☐ the width of the fireplace
☐ from fireplace to second wall
☐ from wall to wall

Then check that the individual measurements add up to the wall-to-wall total. Remember, too, to measure the width of the doors, door frames, windows and window frames.

Measuring accurately For most purposes rooms can be assumed to have right-angled corners and parallel walls that are equal in length and height, though this is rarely the case. If the measurements are only slightly different it is not worth worrying about, but if you are measuring for built-in furniture, you will need a more accurate plan.

7

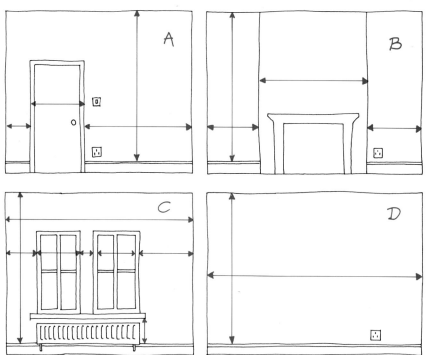

DRAWING ELEVATIONS

The floor sketch gives you the basic dimensions of the room: the next step is to do a plan of each wall, called an elevation. Make a rough sketch of the wall. You already have the widths of each wall from your floor plan; now, measure the height of each wall and the height of features such as doors, windows and chair rails.

Trick of the trade If you're on your own, use a couple of 6ft. canes or dowels to measure elevations. Stand on a chair and hold the poles against the walls; slide them apart to the full height of the room and then tape them together firmly.

Now mark the height of each feature – curtain track, mantelpiece, window and door frame etc – on the taped together poles. Place the poles on the floor, read off the measurements and transfer them to your elevation sketch.

THE FINISHED PLAN

Now transfer the rough sketch measurements for the floor plan and wall elevations onto graph or square paper. **With standard 10-squares-per-inch graph paper,** and a scale of **1 small square=2 inches,** the maximum size room to fit on an 8½in.×11in. piece of paper is approximately 13 feet by 16 feet. For larger rooms, try a larger scale, such as 1 square=1ft.

With 5-squares-per-inch graph paper, a scale of **1 square=5 inches,** the maximum size room to fit on an 8½in.×11in. sheet of paper is approximately 14½ft.×21ft. For larger areas, try a scale of 1 square=1ft.

△ Life-size sample of 10-squares-per-inch graph paper.
▽ 5-squares-per-inch graph paper.

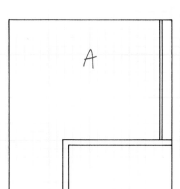

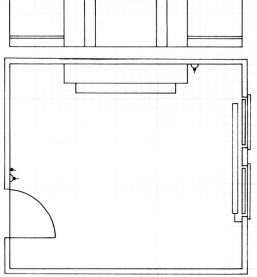

CALCULATING QUANTITIES

How much paint, tiles, wallcovering, etc, to buy depends on the area they are intended to cover. So you need to work out the area of the floor, walls and ceiling before ordering any materials.

Use the elevation drawings to find the area of the walls in a room: multiply the height by the width of each wall and add the totals together.

Use the floor plan to help you estimate both the floor and ceiling areas. To find the area of the floor or ceiling, multiply the length of the room by its width.

If the room is L-shaped, simply divide the floor plan into two rectangles, multiply the width and length of each rectangle and then add them together for the area of the whole room. Use this method for any recess or bay.

SYMBOL SENSE

These are the most common of the standard symbols used on plans drawn up by professionals.

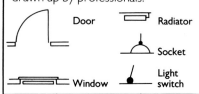

PLANNING YOUR LIVING ROOM

With the pressure on space in today's homes, living rooms often have to accommodate a variety of activities.

Nowadays, living rooms are the place for doing all kinds of things, from entertaining guests to sewing; from watching television to doing homework. But at the same time, the living room is the showcase of your home, somewhere you can express your tastes and display treasured possessions. The way to reconcile these two aspects is through good organization and planning.

ALTERING THE STRUCTURE

Any changes to the basic structure of the living room must be carried out well before you start to decorate. Remodeling varies from simple work you can do yourself to major, expensive changes for which you will need professional help. Common alterations requiring building work include:

☐ blocking or opening up a fireplace
☐ blocking or opening up a doorway
☐ building two rooms into one
☐ moving a partition wall
☐ enlarging or putting in a new window – for example, bay windows
☐ extending the living room – for example, adding a conservatory.

Consider whether the changes are worth the cost and disruption. If you are only planning to stay in your home a couple of years, a cosmetic solution might be a wiser alternative. For instance, instead of blocking up an unused doorway, you could simply disguise it by placing a large piece of furniture in front of it, or turning it into a display alcove.

SERVICES

Installing new wiring or new electrical outlets is also work that should be done at an early stage. Don't finish decorating and then discover that you need more electrical outlets. If you are already engaged in building work, think about adding more outlets at the same time. This will provide you with flexibility when it comes to planning furnishings, TV and stereo arrangements, and also prevent trailing wires that ruin the appearance of the room. You might also consider wiring all the lighting to a central switch by the door, regulated by a dimmer.

LIGHTING

Before you begin to decorate is also the time to decide whether you need to make any changes to the existing lighting set-up. Avoid glaring overhead light; instead create atmospheric pools of light with table lamps, uplighters and spots. Provide a concentrated light source for a work area if you need one. If you want wall-mounted fixtures or concealed downlighters, you should also install these before you start.

▽ *Lighting plan*
A ceiling track with three spotlights provides general illumination in this squarish room. The two table lamps and standard lamp make pools of light for reading, while the picture light and concealed display lights on either side of the fireplace give indirect light.

BEFORE YOU BEGIN

Start by listing all the activities you expect to take place in the living room, now or in the foreseeable future. These may include:

☐ watching television; listening to records
☐ entertaining guests; parties
☐ putting visitors up for the night
☐ reading; quiet study or other hobbies
☐ dining
☐ children's play.

Now look carefully at existing features, furniture, lighting and decoration to decide what you would like to retain and what needs replacing.

☐ Is there a special feature you would like to emphasize?
☐ Would some structural work improve the layout?
☐ Is the furniture right for the room?
☐ Does the lighting work well?
☐ Are there enough electrical outlets – in the right place?
☐ Does the decoration suit your taste and belongings?
☐ Do you need more shelves or cupboard space?

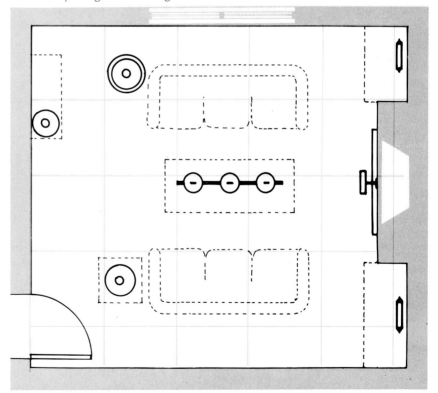

Scale: 1 square = 1 square yard

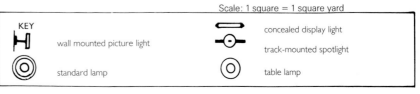

KEY

H⌐ wall mounted picture light

◎ standard lamp

⊖ concealed display light

⊙ track-mounted spotlight

◎ table lamp

FURNISHINGS

Living rooms are all about seating arrangements. There are several guidelines to bear in mind when devising a layout. The first is to identify a focal point. This can be a fireplace, coffee table or a good view. If your room lacks a focus, think about creating one: a group of plants lit by an uplighter; a strategically placed mirror to reflect light or a view; a painting, a beautiful object or fine piece of furniture.

Seating plan Now work out your seating around the focal point. Draw up a scale plan of the room, illustrating doors, windows, electrical outlets and switches, light fixtures, radiators and any features, such as a fireplace or alcove. Measure the furniture you own or would like to buy and draw the shapes to scale on a piece of cardboard. Cut them out and arrange them on the plan of the room until you arrive at the best layout.

Symmetrical or L-shaped arrangements suit most rooms, provided the size and style of the furniture is right. Take a good look at the furniture you have. One piece that is too large or overbearing can ruin the feel of the whole room. Be firm with yourself, if something doesn't look right it might be best to sell it or lend it to friends.

Bear in mind that a three-seater sofa can be a waste of space. Although it may seat two people comfortably, no one likes to sit in the middle. A sofa placed directly in front of a fireplace will block the heat and the view, and create a dead area behind.

Flexibility If you entertain regularly, be sure at least some of your furniture can be moved about easily, and provide upholstered stools for extra seating, and side tables for glasses and plates.

Arranging seating so that everyone can watch TV in comfort, but without the blank screen dominating the room when you are entertaining is often a problem. Try to plan your layout so that chairs and sofas can be turned around or moved so that the emphasis is changed. Another solution is to keep the TV on a wheeled base or trolley that can be pulled out for viewing.

Dining area If your living room must provide space for dining, arrange the furniture so there is a degree of separation between the different areas. A partition or screen might help and an extending table and folding chairs will save on space.

Finishing touches are important. Make room for your treasured possessions, whether they are pictures, objects or a special chair. Your living room should say something about yourself, it should not be a sterile display of 'good taste.'

A DECORATIVE SCHEME

The best starting point for a decorative scheme is often the floor. This is likely to be the most expensive item and will have a dominating effect because of the sheer surface area involved. It will also outlast the paint job, so if you are choosing a carpet, for example, opt for a shade that will suit several different color schemes.

Always plan the decoration for the room as a whole. Don't find your options strictly limited because you have picked out a particularly vivid pattern for the curtains and then can't find anything to go with it. Take your time, especially if you are decorating from scratch.

Collect samples of the colors, patterns and materials you would like to use for curtains, blinds, upholstery, flooring, walls, ceilings and woodwork. Assemble them on a single sheet of paper or cardboard to see how they look together.

STORAGE

If your living room is used for several different activities, maintaining the overall style and atmosphere without sacrificing practicality is largely a question of providing adequate storage. Books, records and ornaments can be displayed on open shelves; other items are best concealed in cabinets.

Built-in cabinets or freestanding units can be used to stow electronic equipment, sewing materials, games or hobbies – anything you don't want on view. A sideboard in a dining area can be an attractive way of storing table linen, cutlery, drinks and glasses.

A trolley is also very useful – as a mobile liquor cabinet or to carry the TV or video equipment. When not required, it can simply be wheeled out of sight. And if your living room is also the children's play area, a deep wicker basket with a lid, or a wooden chest would make a stylish home for toys at the end of the day.

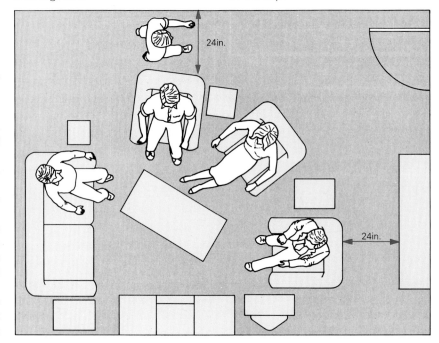

24in.

24in.

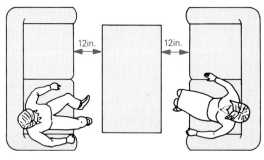

12in.   12in.

16in.   14in.   20in.

△ **Space to pass**
Allow a minimum of 24in. for someone to walk into or around a room without having to squeeze past people already seated.

◁ **Knee room**
Make sure there is at least 12in. between the edges of seats and the coffee table so that people can stand up and sit comfortably.

◁ **Standard seating**
These measurements are the typical height of a coffee table and the depth and height of an armchair.

10

THE HEART OF THE LIVING ROOM

The key to creating a welcoming living room is to have a focal point – something that invites people to gather around and relax.

A living room without a focal point is a room without life. Family and friends need something to gather around when they're sitting down, otherwise they tend to feel uneasy and 'lost' – even in a modest-size room.

Without a focal point, it is almost impossible to plan the rest of a room successfully. A well-planned room has nothing to do with the quantity of furniture. It is easy to make the mistake of cramming a room full of tables and chairs but still not manage to give it a focal point. More often, it is a question of planning your layout to make the most of the room's good points and minimize the bad ones.

By rearranging the furniture and re-thinking the lighting, you can give a room a 'heart.'

The appeal of a fire In the past, the hearth was always the heart of the living room. There's something about the warm, flickering light of a fire that draws you towards it – even if you're not too cold.

But many modern houses don't have a traditional log or coal fire. Instead, they rely on gas or electric fires, which by themselves can look uninviting, particularly when switched off. And some homes have no fireplace at all.

The temptation is just to turn to the TV set as the source of life and interest, then arrange things accordingly. But although this is fine when the TV is on and everyone wants to watch it, the results are unsettling when it's switched off, and the blank screen sits there watching you.

Home is where the hearth is
Traditionally, the fireplace has always been the focal point of the living room – few things compare with the inviting glow of flickering flames.

ALTERNATIVE FOCAL POINTS

If there is no fireplace, you need to look carefully at what else the room has to offer, then decide where to place the emphasis. Two favorite alternatives are coffee tables and picture windows, but before you consider their pros and cons, do remember that often a combination of focal points works best. For example, the focus can change easily to a coffee table when the fire is unlit or the curtains are drawn.

Coffee tables The classic focal point for an otherwise featureless room, a coffee table serves as the center around which seating can be clustered. You've probably already got one somewhere but ask yourself if it is large enough to do the job — can the family really gather around it? If you can't find one the right size consider butting two square or oblong tables together.

The beauty of coffee tables is that they are easy to decorate. Make sure yours is interesting and eyecatching — use flowers or houseplants, books, candles, collections of seashells, a bowl of fruit or attractive ashtrays — and change it whenever the mood takes you.

Try to make the table display a personal one, to avoid the anonymous, 'waiting-room' style of decoration. (Try to keep it from becoming a permanent depository for children's toys, and dirty cups. It is the one piece of furniture that attracts attention — and inspection!)

Windows A wonderful view is too precious to ignore. You may decide to plan the seating so that the outdoors is part of everyone's view when seated, and so that your visitors' attention is drawn to it the moment they enter the room.

Set off the view with blinds if the windows are narrow — or pretty curtains

A floor outlet lets you plug in a table or standard lamp almost anywhere without having to put up with a trailing wire. Fitted with a childproof hinged cover plate, with a satin brass or matte chrome finish, it can be stood on safely when not in use.

◁ *Coffee table centerpiece*
When a room lacks a 'natural' focal point, create your own with a coffee table and arrange the seating around it. Notice, here, how the table lamp and decorations help to attract the eye.

1 square = 1 square yard

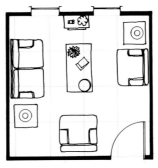

▽ *Creating a pool of light*
This alternative arrangement based on a three-piece set makes more use of the window view as a focal point. By night, the coffee table becomes the main center of interest – lit by a ceiling downlighter instead of a lamp, with a recessed eyeball downlighter making the painting a secondary focal point.

tied back to each side if they are wide.

Whatever the focal point, don't forget to make your furniture arrangement inviting. Often there isn't enough room to do this successfully with a three-piece set so, if you are thinking of changing your furniture, consider the alternative scheme of two sofas placed at right angles or facing each other. Research shows that the right-angle arrangement puts everyone at ease immediately and creates the perfect place for a coffee table within easy reach of everyone's seat.

A ROOM FOR ALL SEASONS

Like a garden, the truly comfortable living room can change with the seasons.

In summer In a room where the fire is the natural focal point, you need to think about those long summer days (and evenings) when it won't be lit. If you want the general atmosphere to be light and airy, pull your furniture back from the fireplace and aim to make better use of the room as a whole. A coffee table makes an excellent alternative focal point when illuminated by a gentle pool of light from a downlighter set into the ceiling.

To stop the fireplace itself from looking dull and gloomy, surround it with plants, fill the grate with pine-cones or place a treasured item – such as a decorative screen – in front. Here, the TV has been moved to the wall where the camera is positioned so it can be watched from both sofas but doesn't dominate the room.

In winter Coziness and warmth are the main considerations, so group your sofas and chairs around the fire, with the coffee table playing a secondary role.

Now you can move the TV to one side of the fireplace so both focal points are close together and you can watch in comfort in front of the warm, flickering glow of the fire.

1 square = 1 square yard

Summer freshness, winter warmth
In summer (top), the fireplace plays more of a background role. Open up your seating plan to give people air and space, grouping them around a pleasantly decorated coffee table. But don't forget the empty hearth – plants or dried flowers will prevent it from looking gloomy.

In winter (above), coziness becomes the order of the day (floor plan right). Regroup seating around the fire and move the TV to this side of the room.

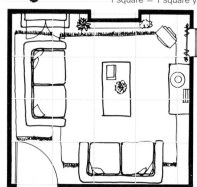

A ROOM WITH A VIEW

An attractive view can provide a satisfying focal point by day, particularly if you choose a simple, undistracting window treatment. But don't forget that at night you will no longer be able to see the view and will need to make some other arrangement.

Here, the room is planned by day to make the best of the group of large plants, the balcony and the view beyond. The sofa faces outwards and the swivel chair can face in or out.

By night, clever lighting emphasizes the indoor plants, while a light on the balcony creates a 'view' outside. A floor uplighter – like a tin can with a bulb in it – is placed below the main group of plants to focus attention on them, and cast dramatic, leafy shadows over the ceiling. Another plant outside is picked out with a weatherproof spotlight mounted above the doors, making the balcony part of the focal point.

Night and day
At night (right) plants are lit up, both indoors and out, to become the focus of interest.

By day (below) the owner of this apartment can enjoy the view, while the indoor plants provide interest and a visual link. The TV is placed to one side so it does not spoil the view or create a glare.

1 square = 1 square yard

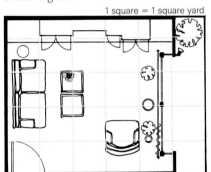

◁ **Television center**
In this attic room the emphasis is on the TV, which forms part of a built-in shelving system. When the rafters were boarded in, a recess was created above the bookshelves for a VCR, and it also provides attractive windowsills for plants and ornaments – alternative viewpoints when the set is switched off.

The L-shaped seating arrangement in this rather narrow room offers an inviting corner to curl up with a book under the lamp.

▷ **Behind closed doors**
Here, the problem of what to do with the TV was overcome by filling one wall with wooden shelves, drawers and cabinets; the center section houses both TV and VCR behind a pair of doors. The formality of the units is emphasized by the arrangement of pictures.

When the doors are closed on the TV, the focal point changes. The seating is grouped to make the most of the enclosed fireplace and gives a glimpse of the outside to those sitting on the sofa. From the chair there is a 'borrowed' view in the mirror.

◁ **Effective paint**
This corner used to house a large TV in a nasty imitation wood finish, VCR and masses of tangled wires. The inexpensive solution was to build low cabinets between the fireplace and window wall, angled at the window end to make a deeper shelf. The VCR is now hidden in the cabinets; the TV, minus its legs, sits above. The TV and cabinets were painted pale gray and then rag rolled and sponged in blue and yellow, picking up the colors in the room.

DINING AREAS IN LIVING ROOMS

One comfortable room that combines both a living and a dining area can be an ideal arrangement.

The most used room in the house – the living/dining room – should be designed for comfort and convenience. This is where you spend time sitting, relaxing or watching TV, and where you eat evening meals and entertain.

Depending on the shape of the room and how it is decorated and furnished, it can be treated as a single room where the living and dining areas are integrated, or planned so that the two areas are separate.

Dividing the two areas The room may be divided physically by a change in shape, floor level or by an archway. Lighting can be used to change the emphasis in the two areas, or you can create the same effect with decoration, using different paint, wallcovering and floor coverings to make a definite boundary.

Another way to divide the room is with furniture, perhaps with a series of low-level cabinets that open out into the dining area or with a sofa facing towards the living room area.

Unifying the room The alternative approach is to treat the room as a single entity. Use the same decorative finishes throughout, linking the two sections with details such as a wallcovering border, or using the same fabric for the main curtains and the tablecloth. The dining area will also look less separate if you choose dining chairs that can be used for extra seating in the living room area.

LIVING/DINING ROOM LAYOUT

Where you locate each area depends largely on the shape of the room. There may be an alcove, a narrow end, or the short leg of an L-shape that is ideal for a table and chairs. Otherwise the obvious place is close to the kitchen. Modern houses are often designed with the eating area as an integral part of the living room. In older houses, the wall between the living and dining rooms may be opened up to give more space with the dining area at one end.

Practical space
This dining area flows easily from the adjoining living area. The simple decor, an off-white color partnered with a neutral rug, paves the way for more colorful accents. A stone fireplace wall partially divides the space creating a more natural division. Pretty lace place mats dress up a traditional dining table.

STORAGE SENSE

Any dining area needs to have enough storage space to house your china, glass, table linen and cutlery.

Old-fashioned sideboards are very useful in living/dining rooms, being slightly higher than their modern equivalents, which has a dual advantage: they are the perfect height for carving and serving food from as well as providing more storage space.

Low-level cabinets can be used for storage and as room dividers, while taller closets, possibly glass-fronted, make the best use of floor space.

LIGHTING

A lot of activities other than sitting and eating take place in a living/dining room, so it requires flexible lighting.

It is important to work out exactly what you use the room for and how much time you spend doing what. Identify what you do where as well as what sort of moods you want to create.

Task lighting for reading and to illuminate areas such as the stereo and the

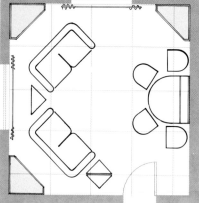

TV are a good idea, and so is a dimmer switch. You need sufficient lighting over the table so you can see what you're eating but at the same time, the light should be subtle and flattering to faces and food. Avoid non-adjustable overhead fixtures, which may be in the wrong place if you decide to move the furniture around. Table or floor lamps close by give a softer glow and can also serve as task lights when the table is used for other activities.

△ **Corner wise**
The three corner cabinets have a surprising amount of storage space.

During meals, the sofas can be moved back and the table opened out into the room (see plan, below). When not in use, the drop-leaf table is pushed against the wall and the dining chairs are turned around (see left).

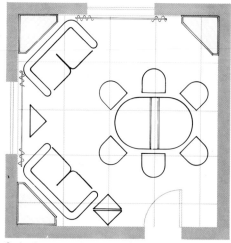

Scale: 1 square = 1 square yard

18

A flexible lighting scheme should include an adjustable light for the dining table, such as a rise-and-fall pendant or wall lights controlled by a dimmer switch, and some general light with plenty of outlets for task lighting and table lamps in the living area.

wall light

rise-and-fall

uplighter

table lamp

▽ *Folding solution*

Here, instead of the drop-leaf, a long modern table that folds in half lengthwise has been chosen.

As shown in the diagram right, it opens out into a full-size dining table and when folded, it makes a handsome console table, pushed back against the wall. An elegant dining chair fits neatly at either end and additional seats can be carried in from other rooms when needed.

19

SOFAS AND CHAIRS

As the living/dining room is used for more than one purpose, versatility should be a priority. Space may be tight, so choose chairs and sofas that aren't too bulky. If the living room furniture has to be pushed back to make room for the dining table when it is extended, make sure everything has casters or is light enough to be carried.

TABLES

Rectangular or oval tables that can be made longer or smaller are perfect for dual-purpose rooms, provided there is somewhere to store a detachable leaf when it is not required. If you don't have the room, choose a drop-leaf table, or one where the leaves are attached at either end and can be pushed into the body of the table to reduce its size.

The dining table is likely to become a social center for a wide range of activities – conversation, homework, games and hobbies as well as mealtime get-togethers – so the table has to survive everyday wear and tear and still look its best when you are entertaining.

A table top that is durable is the most practical choice. Laminated plastic immediately comes to mind – it is tough and easy to keep clean, and although somewhat utilitarian in appearance, can be dressed up for formal occasions. Natural wood, such as oak, beech or pine, looks good and can be treated with a polyurethane seal to give a hard-wearing, natural-looking finish.

A polished wooden table needs to be safeguarded from heat, spills and scratches with a thick tablecloth. If the tabletop is particularly good, use a felt pad under the tablecloth for extra protection.

Entertaining As soon as your guests arrive and see the dining table laid for a meal it becomes the center of attention, so it is worth dressing it up for special occasions. Even the shabbiest old table – a junk shop find, a picnic table, or an old flush door supported by a pair of decorators' trestles – can be transformed with a smart linen tablecloth and a pair of candlesticks.

CHAIRS

Dining chairs don't have to match as long as there are some common visual elements such as color, shape, upholstery and so on. Conventional chairs, tucked in position around a dining table that is not being used, can look very formal. Instead, choose chairs that can do double duty – as extra seating in the living area, kitchen or bedrooms. Chairs that stack or fold flat, canvas director's chairs and even stools are also ideal.

Comfort and practicality are as important as appearance when choosing chairs. With a permanent dining area, fixed banquette seating either side of the table makes good use of space but it can be a rather uncomfortable arrangement. Compromise with a bench on one side, and chairs opposite.

▷ *Simple color scheme*
Storage plays a large part in the success of this living/dining room. The storage unit has cupboards and drawers for china, cutlery and tablecloths, with open shelves and illuminated glazed cupboard sections for displaying treasured possessions.

Sleek, matching chrome furniture upholstered in pale gray against a background of peach carpets and walls, creates a feeling of space.

Scale: 1 square = 1 square yard

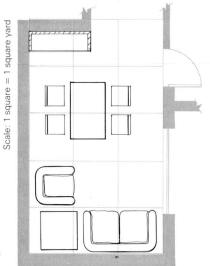

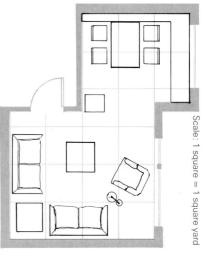

◁ **Through room**
This airy living room was designed with a dining alcove off the main seating area. The two zones are clearly defined by the change in shape but are held together, visually, by the use of the same curtain treatment and carpet.

During meals, the desk under the window becomes an extra surface for serving food and the rise-and-fall light can be lowered over the dining table.

Scale: 1 square = 1 square yard

BRIGHT IDEA

A folding screen forms a light and adjustable divider between the seating and dining area in a small living room. This makes the dining area cozier while you are eating and hides a messy table when you are relaxing after the meal.

This openwork screen divides the room without cutting out the light. Its pale color goes well with the stripped and sealed wooden floor and simple beech dining table and bentwood chairs.

Painted antique screens can often be found in secondhand shops, or you could make your own: construct two or three rectangular wooden frames, hinge them together and drape with fabric to match your curtains or upholstery.

△ Casual comfort

This living/dining room is decorated simply and comfortably. Wood-crafted furniture pieces complement a shiny wood floor. Abstract-patterned draperies, along with yellow papered walls, add color and interest.

▷ Serving hatch

Easy access to the kitchen is necessary for serving food and clearing away dishes.

This serving hatch is extra wide and provides a permanent link between the kitchen and dining area, allowing the cook to be included in conversation. Bright accessories and hand-painted ceramic tile add accent to a white kitchen.

EXPANDED LIVING ROOMS

Combine the traditional living room and family room into a Great Room.

In traditional homes, expanded living rooms are divided by doors that can be folded back on themselves to combine the two rooms into a single larger space. These doors have the advantage of allowing great flexibility since, with the doors open, the two rooms can be combined almost instantly – for a Christmas party, perhaps. In some houses, however, the front and back rooms remain entirely separate.

Traditionally, the living room was reserved for 'best' use, a room in which to receive visitors. The family room was set aside for watching television or for children's play.

With today's more informal lifestyles – and the ease with which large rooms can now be kept warm – many people find that a single, Great Room is more appropriate to their needs.

Where doors were a part of the original design, this is fairly easy to achieve. The doors can be removed entirely – or a compromise reached whereby solid doors are replaced by glazed ones that make the division seem less complete.

Two small, separate living areas are often best combined by removing the dividing wall – but remember to check whether the wall is loadbearing before it is removed or altered. A squared-off or arched opening, dividing doors, or some form of temporary or removable partition, could be installed to enable you to enjoy the best of both worlds: separate rooms or a single one.

Open expanse
The large, open space of this Great Room makes it perfect for entertaining. Special areas for dining, watching TV or quiet relaxation also make it a comfortable setting for family moments. A brick fireplace wall divides the living area and the rest of the home.

◁ ▽ **On a formal note**
With only an elegant arch to
divide them, the expanded
living room in this home
serves as a sitting and TV
room. By positioning the
television in one end of the
room (left), the front part
(below) becomes a more
formal living room.

   Both 'ends' of the room are
simply decorated, with a
mixture of traditional and
antique furniture set against
plain walls, carpeting and
upholstery. The sole
exception is the window
dressing where patterned
fabric forms full, rich curtains,
topped by pinch-pleated
pelmets.

   The single decorative
theme creates a feeling of
unity between the elaborate
windows at each end.

MAKING CHOICES

The way you make use of expanded living rooms is governed by your lifestyle, the size of your home and, of course, the way the house was built.

What are your needs? If you have a large, naturally untidy family, would it be a good idea to keep one half reserved for 'best' use? That way, the arrival of unexpected guests won't throw the entire household into a state of panic as a frantic rush begins to make the living room look presentable. If this is the case, it's best to ensure that the living room is entirely separate, so that the family room's clutter doesn't gradually creep over the boundaries. If necessary, install a partition (perhaps a movable one) where there was none before.

Is the kitchen large enough to accommodate a table? If not, you may want to use part of the Great Room for eating. A small kitchen table may suffice for family use. Select a larger table if you intend to entertain guests.

Does the house pose any limitations?
If the living and family rooms are very small, combining them into a single larger space may be the only option that makes sense. In contrast, bigger living rooms that have been combined may feel too large for comfort.

You may feel that you need to maintain a division in order to keep the functions of the rooms separate. If you like formal entertaining, for example, a small dining room and an equally small living room may be much more useful than a single room, however much more spacious it may be.

Considering your options It is important to ascertain whether a dividing wall is loadbearing or not. If it is, removing it entirely (or partially) is problematic since a supporting beam must be installed to carry the load. Consider your options carefully, and bear in mind the original layout envisaged by the builders of your home – a gently curved arch may be more in keeping with the style

△ *Traditional elegance*
Large, well-proportioned, expanded rooms lend themselves to a traditional style of decoration. Here, one section of the room is used as a living room, while the other serves as a dining room. A decorative opening divides the two.

of the room than a squared-off opening. Decorative moldings, architraves, or corbels not only enhance the look of the arch, they also protect it from accidental damage. Erecting a partition where none existed before is, obviously, less difficult.

A useful compromise may be to arrange matters so that the expanded living room can be temporarily divided (by means of a movable screen or curtain), or partially divided (perhaps by arranging a piece of furniture across the opening). However, in some situations – that of a messy family, for instance – this may be self-defeating.

THE BEST OF BOTH WORLDS

Apart from completely removable divisions, there are many ways of separating the parts of an expanded living room so that, when necessary, they can still be combined into one.

Folding doors were often installed for this reason and can be replaced fairly easily if they have been removed – as can conventional doors that hang from side hinges. Folding, bi-fold and sliding doors all save on floor space – but remember to allow sufficient wall space for sliding doors to open.

Doors are available in a great variety of styles and finishes. Fully or partially glazed types allow both rooms to benefit from an extended view and make small rooms appear larger. Paneled doors suit period homes; flush doors are better suited to more modern houses.

△ *Through room*
It's often best to decorate an expanded living area similarly. The floor and wall treatments unite these rooms and the ornate mirror in the foreground echoes that in the dining room.

▽ *Flexible division*
If rooms are not to be permanently divided, thick curtains hung across an opening can be drawn when required. A pair of armchairs placed so that they form a barrier reinforce the division.

Scale: 1 square = 1 square yard

26

◁ *Vertical blinds*
In a modern setting, streamlined vertical blinds can be used both as a flexible room divider and as a covering for large windows. In order to ensure that they hang well, each of the vertical louvers that make up the blind can incorporate an individual weight in a sealed pocket – or the weights can be linked by a continuous chain.

▽ *Letting the light through*
A partition constructed entirely (or partially) of doors allows expanded living rooms to be opened up and closed off in a matter of seconds. If solid doors would cut out too much light, fully or partially glazed types can be used.
  Cut glass stars add an individual touch to the mahogany doors shown here.

27

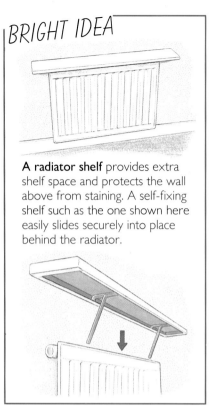

A radiator shelf provides extra shelf space and protects the wall above from staining. A self-fixing shelf such as the one shown here easily slides securely into place behind the radiator.

△ **Traditional feel**
In order to produce an extremely spacious living room, almost all traces of the divider between the original rooms have been removed; all that remains is a narrow supporting beam at ceiling height.
   Although the color scheme, furniture and soft furnishings do not change, a pair of armchairs visually divide the living area.

◁ **Decorative arch**
By removing as much of the original dividing wall as possible, a squared-off opening has been made in this extended living area. The high ceiling and balcony create a spacious effect.

OPEN-PLAN LIVING

If they are to work successfully, open-plan rooms need careful thought and planning.

Although open-plan living may not be to everyone's taste, many of today's apartments are built with such a layout. Because of the relatively small size of many new houses, the living and dining rooms are often combined, and sometimes the hall, stairs and kitchen are also part of the same layout. The absence of dividing walls allows a limited floor area to appear roomier so that the inhabitants feel less cramped.

On the other hand, large modern houses can also have an open layout. Dividing walls on the ground floor of many older homes have been removed in order to combine one or more rooms into a single, spacious living area.

The pros and cons Open-plan living has several distinct advantages. In the first place, it is particularly suited to an informal lifestyle, where different activities are not confined to separate rooms. If, for example, you and your family are not keen on formal entertaining, but like guests to mingle with the entire family and, perhaps, its clutter, then an open layout creates a relaxed and informal atmosphere.

In a small space, the absence of clearly defined rooms produces an illusion of spaciousness – and it is also true that walls do take up valuable floor space. In a larger home, a layout that is not sectioned off creates a luxurious feeling of unlimited space with unlimited possibilities.

In contrast, though, an open living area implies a sacrifice of privacy as well as peace and quiet. It is more difficult for members of the family to pursue different activities if they cannot physically separate themselves from each other. Teenagers, for instance, may want to listen to noisy records while their parents would prefer somewhere quiet. In addition, decor and furniture are more difficult to arrange so that the space is functional and visually unified.

A clever compromise

Partitions create distinct activity areas in this studio apartment. The living area is cut off from the bedroom by sliding doors, and from the kitchen by shelves. A peninsula unit used for meals separates kitchen and work area.

△ **A modern home**
A single decorating scheme unites this studio. The same gray and white colors are used throughout, and a tiled floor flows continuously through each area.

A large, strategically placed laminate island can serve many functions. Not only is it appropriate for use as a serving table, but also as a breakfast bar and storage space.

Scale: 1 square = 1 square yard

◁ **An open-plan layout**
In many newly built houses, the entire ground floor has an open-plan layout. In this example, the living and dining rooms are combined into a single living space. However, a wall separates the front door and the living area, thus creating a small but useful hallway. The small kitchen is either a separate room or it is separated from the main living area by kitchen units.

BRIGHT IDEA

A wet bar with overhead glass storage makes entertaining easy in an open studio layout.

A FEELING OF SPACE

An open-plan layout can be successfully created even if this was not what the architect originally intended. Knocking down a nonloadbearing wall can be a relatively simple matter, although it's always best to seek professional advice. All traces of the wall can be removed, and the rooms totally united.

However, a loadbearing wall is essential to the structure of the house and cannot be removed entirely. A reinforced joist or beam must be installed to carry the weight of the floor or roof above. Since the joist and the side pillars on which it rests will be visible, some traces of the obsolete wall have to remain. An arch is often installed in such an opening, so that the room appears long and thin, with a 'waist' in the middle.

Before taking any action, though, consider the character and proportions of the rooms. Period houses can be ruined if interior walls are indiscriminately knocked down. So long as it is done with sensitivity, an eye to proportion and respect for the original structure of the house, however, there is no reason why some rooms, at least, cannot be combined.

UNITY OF STYLE

Planning the decor of an open living room can be complicated, since you need to combine an overall impression of unity with a suitable atmosphere for each activity area.

Overall cohesion is best created by the use of the same (or similar) wall and floorcoverings throughout the room. Use lighting, furniture and accent colors in accessories and furnishings to alter subtly the mood in, say, the living and dining areas.

If the room has a natural break (for example, along the line of a wall that has been removed), it is easier to change the color scheme and flooring in the two parts and still avoid a disjointed end result.

Where you decide to place items of furniture requires special attention. There must be enough space to allow people to move around easily, but without creating 'dead,' unused areas in the middle of the room or in one leg of an L-shape. List all the activities that are likely to take place in the room and group the furniture to form relatively separate activity areas. Rugs can form effective focal points and furniture can be positioned to section off areas.

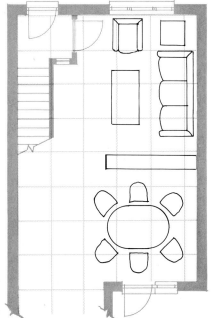

Scale: 1 square = 1 square yard

▽ *A new arrangement*
Since space is limited in this open plan, a see-through shelving unit serves both to display plants and ornaments and as a room divider. This separates the dining area to some extent but at the same time ensures that the two sections of the room do not feel uncomfortably claustrophobic.

DIVIDING THE SPACE

If you are unhappy with an existing open layout, a large space can be subdivided into two smaller ones.

A partition not only increases privacy in the newly-created rooms but it also makes decoration easier as the new rooms can be tailored for their intended use.

Before you forge ahead and build a permanent divider, or buy a freestanding partition that may not fit the bill, experiment with an improvised divider to make certain that the new arrangement will be to your liking. The dividing line needs to be carefully placed so that it does not cut across a window, make a room disagreeably dark, slice an elegant plastered ceiling in two or obstruct movement around the room.

◁ *An open divider*
This pass-through visually separates and hides any mess in the kitchen without totally cutting off the kitchen from the dining area.

▽ *Partial division*
Although several walls have been removed in this modern home, part of one wall has been left intact to screen cooking activity from the sitting area.

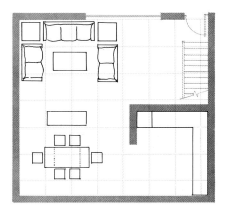

Scale: 1 square = 1 square yard

CHOOSING A PARTITION

The least permanent way of dividing up a living area is by arranging the furniture – a sofa, sideboard or shelving unit – so that it forms a barrier. The only proviso here is that the back of the piece of furniture must be presentable – and this is often not the case with furniture designed to be placed along a wall.

Floor-to-ceiling curtains can muffle sound and create a soft look. Because they will be seen from both sides, use either a double thickness or a sheer fabric. Another possibility is to hang vertical or mini blinds from the ceiling. (Since mini blinds are not made in large widths, you may have to hang two or three next to one another.) Finally, folding or sliding screens are available in many different styles – or you can make your own. They are easily moved around to suit the occasion.

A permanent dividing wall is not difficult to build since it need be no more substantial than a wood frame covered with Sheetrock. A half-height wall may be the answer in a smallish room, providing privacy without complete division.

Sliding doors can form an entire partition in themselves, or they can be incorporated in a partition wall.

▽ *Furniture as a room divider*
Arranging the furniture can be difficult. Here, a long, low sideboard has been positioned along a line separating the dining and living areas. The seating has also been rearranged to form an L-shape with a two-seater sofa screening the hall area and front door.

Boxing-in the radiators to match the dining table and chairs makes them part of the overall decor rather than necessary evils.

BRIGHT IDEA

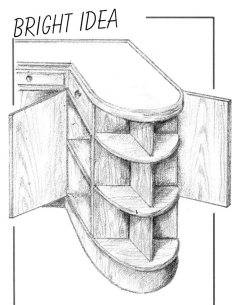

Two-way access A double set of doors on kitchen units between an open plan's kitchen/dining room means that dishes and cutlery are easily reached from both rooms, making setting the table and emptying the dishwasher quicker and easier. One side – preferably the one opening onto the kitchen – can be left open for even easier access.

◁ **Studio living**
The strategic use of sofa beds and fitted storage units turns this room into a complete living space.

Scatter cushions disguise the main bed, which is framed by built-in storage units. The sofa converts into a second bed; such units often incorporate floor-level storage space.

A table and strip light divide the space. As well as providing a work space, they can also be used for dining.

▽ **Light and airy**
Plain white walls enhance the spaciousness of this combined living and dining room. The two areas are also brought together visually by white and off-white furniture and common floorcovering.

USING ROOM DIVIDERS

A room divider can help to make the most of any living room, whether large or small.

Room dividers come in a great variety of shapes and sizes and can be useful in the smallest or largest of living rooms. They range from temporary to more permanent structures and you can either purchase one ready-made or improvise your own arrangement.

The type you choose will obviously depend on the function it has to perform, as well as the size and decorative style of the room. So begin by carefully considering your reasons for wanting one. Do you want to create different activity areas within a single, perhaps relatively small, room? Or do you have a large living space that would become more inviting and cozy if it were sectioned off into relatively private corners?

Do you want the divider to be a permanent structure in the room – or should it be movable to allow flexibility if, for example, you want to use the whole room for a party or family gathering?

How completely should it divide the room? In some instances, particularly in smaller spaces, it is often best to choose a style that is open so that it is still possible to see through from one part of the room to another.

Partial division
A bookcase creates a natural division between kitchen and living area. The lighted aquarium offers visual interest. Floor level changes emphasize the difference between the two rooms.

MAKING CHOICES

Partitions can be very dominant features in a room. So before going ahead with major building projects or purchases, it's a good idea to try out a makeshift screening arrangement to see if it is comfortable to live with.

Permanent dividers Fixed bookshelves can have a solid back for a total division; open shelves naturally create a more open partition. A low wall, or kitchen base units, divide a room up to waist level. And although they are permanent features, folding and sliding doors are extremely flexible.

Temporary dividers are flexible and need not be expensive. As well as a huge range of screens, consider the simple solution of arranging furniture to create a division. Curtains or blinds can be hung from the ceiling to be drawn when needed.

▷ Open partition
A combination kitchen/living room often benefits from some form of division. This need be no more than a kitchen base unit between the two areas.

Here, a large storage unit provides extra countertop space on the kitchen side and a large cupboard for storing utensils, napkins and the like on the dining room side.

▽ Mantel wall
A custom-crafted fireplace wall is a grand way to divide a large living area. Creating separate spaces behind and to each side, the fireplace becomes the focal point.

△ Open-plan
Dividers create distinct activity areas in this large living area. A low wall is backed by a sofa to form a dining area, and a sideboard in front of the second sofa defines the other side of the seating area.

◁ More complete division
To create greater privacy, floor-to-ceiling partitions have been installed above the existing dividers.

The low wall has been topped by framed panels of perforated hardboard screening, while open shelving and cabinets have been added to low closets in the foreground.

37

SCREEN PLAY

A freestanding screen is a flexible type of room divider in terms of style, size and portability.

Because they are not usually attached to the wall, floor, or ceiling, screens can be easily moved around. In addition, of course, most screens can be folded back against a wall when not required. And since the individual panels which make up a screen are generally clipped, hinged, or bolted together, you can create a partition as large or small as you need.

Many different shapes and styles are available, and you can also make your own to coordinate exactly with the style of the room. Apart from antique screens, there are many modern versions made from solid or slatted wood or cane, or plastic or metal for high-tech designs. Japanese-style screens, where paper is attached to a wooden frame, are widely available; for a romantic, translucent effect, consider stretching a lacy or sheer fabric over a frame.

BRIGHT IDEA

Making a screen is not difficult. This screen was made by hinging together three hardboard-faced doors (available from do-it-yourself (DIY) home center stores). Such a simple screen can be decorated to match the decor.

▽ *Color coordination*
By making a screen yourself, you can choose a color and shape to match your decorating scheme.

Here, a three-panel screen with an elegant arched top has been covered with the same fabric used for the upholstery. As a result, the screen becomes an integral part of the room's overall color scheme.

By placing furniture on both sides of the screen, any possibility of knocking it over is drastically reduced – an important consideration in a household that includes elderly people or boisterous young children or pets.

THREE STAGES TO A PERFECT LIVING ROOM

Build up gradually so that at every stage you have a pleasant living room.

It is rare that anyone can move into a new home, look at the bare surroundings and go straight out to buy furniture, furnishings and accessories in one fell swoop. Most people are restricted by their budget – and you may have children and feel it's not worth having 'good' furniture until they've grown up.

Nevertheless, you have to start with some furniture, and there are two ways to approach this, depending on your circumstances. First consider how long you plan to stay in your new home. If you are a first-time buyer, statistics point to your moving within five years. If, on the other hand, it is your second (or third) move – to a real family home

– you'll probably be there for much longer. No matter which of these two pictures fits you, planning a staged development is a practical approach to achieving the room scheme you want, whether over a short, medium, or long time span.

SHORT TERM
Stage 1 If it's your first home, go for the basics and keep things simple. You'll need a coffee table – choose one big enough to serve your seating arrangement and buy the best you can afford, as they take a lot of wear. For extra seating look for something inexpensive yet stylish, such as director's chairs.

Storage is vital – as much as you can afford. Adjustable shelving that's part of a modular system will fit in with a planned scheme. Paint the walls white or creamy beige; at the window drape inexpensive fabric or hang a blind. Perhaps sand and varnish floorboards.

Stage 2 Within nine months, review the flooring – either replace old carpet or buy a rug. Review window coverings again, replace or buy curtains or blinds. Consider your walls and perhaps liven them up with some color – either sponged or marbled paint, or a wallcovering. Plan a lighting scheme and get started on it.

Stage 3 Within 18 months, complete your lighting scheme and add those extras that dress the room: perhaps another small table, a comfortable chair and more storage units. Hang a few prints, or make a display of favorite items.

First-stage style
This city apartment is furnished with basic necessities – a comfortable sofa and stylish table and lamp. The next step would be flooring – either wall-to-wall carpeting or a large rug – and lighting, possibly wallwashers. Some extra chairs would be a logical addition, too.

BRIGHT IDEA

Wood design A simple and inexpensive way to give real character to a sanded floor is to use different shades of varnish.

For a covering pattern, apply several coats of pale varnish to provide a surface over the whole floor. Then mark off the walls into equal divisions about 12in. apart and join up the marks on opposite walls to form a square grid. You can do this easily by stretching a length of string that has been rubbed in chalk between the marks; flick the taut string to get a chalk line. Brush on darker varnish to create a checkerboard effect.

LONG-TERM PLANNING

When you move into your second or third home, your planning considerations are bound to be very different from those that were paramount in your first home.

First, you probably have quite a lot of furniture that has to be housed. Then there may very well be more people to be accommodated: children of various ages and their clutter can take up a lot of space.

On the other hand, time is on your side. So – don't rush, but plan over as much as five or six years to arrive at your ideal room scheme.

Stage 1 If you can't stand the walls, strip the covering if necessary and paint them a warm neutral shade. Spend your money on flooring – buy carpeting or perhaps sand and stain the floorboards and purchase a large area rug.

You'll almost certainly have to invest in new curtains or blinds, so that is perhaps the point to start your new color scheme. And if your new scheme clashes with the remainders of your old one – perhaps the upholstery fabric – improvise. If you can, make some new slipcovers, or use inexpensive soft fabric as a throwover – a rug or Indian bedspread would be good choices. Look for natural, undyed fabric that can be wrapped over and tucked into the seating. It can look surprisingly effective and stylish.

Stage 2 After a couple of years, gradually withdraw some of the old furniture – use it elsewhere – and replace it with some new pieces.

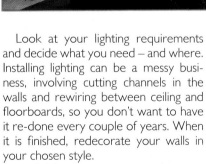

Look at your lighting requirements and decide what you need – and where. Installing lighting can be a messy business, involving cutting channels in the walls and rewiring between ceiling and floorboards, so you don't want to have it re-done every couple of years. When it is finished, redecorate your walls in your chosen style.

Stage 3 After four to six years, buy anything you feel is still missing in the way of furniture and make a point of putting together your finishing touches. Take a good look at the decorations and freshen up anything that looks rather tired. In particular, if you installed blinds or simple curtains when you first moved in, now is perhaps the time to dress the windows more elaborately.

Family progression

The sunny family room shown on this and the opposite page looks comfortable at each of its progressive stages. In the first stage (far left) simple yellow curtains hang from poles. Off-white painted walls provide an inexpensive neutral backdrop that can be easily touched up if it gets scuffed and scraped by children. Main seating is a chesterfield: director's chairs are a carry-over from apartment dwelling days.

In Stage 2 (left) chairs have been replaced by a relatively inexpensive sofa. A rug under the new coffee table and soft primrose walls add coziness, while a good mirror has found a home over the fireplace. A table lamp is more in keeping with the room than the replaced standard lamp.

The third stage (below) has achieved a pleasing symmetry with upholstered chesterfields placed either side of the fireplace. Elegant swags and jabots top the windows where the curtains are held with coordinated tiebacks. The two alcoves have matching cabinets and shelves.

△ ◁ City slick

The pictures on this page show how a slick city style lends itself especially well to advancing by stages. Modular furniture can be bought by degrees, as the budget allows.

The second stage (above) is already a thoroughly comfortable room. Storage in the alcove houses a growing amount of city-living essentials, and has been painted to match the coffee table that was one of the first purchases. Carpeting, a first-stage buy, has been refined by the addition of the rug used to define the working area. First steps in the lighting scheme provide the work area with its own overhead light.

By the time Stage 3 (shown on the left) is reached, the whole scheme takes on a more permanent air. Solid, built-in furniture fills the alcoves on both sides of the chimney; one unit serves as a desk area, replacing the table shown in Stage 2. The carpet – possibly showing signs of wear – has been transferred to a bedroom and the floorboards sanded and attractively stained and sealed. A sleek glass coffee table allows an uninterrupted view of the stylish rug lying in front of the recovered sofa. The window has been dressed with a smart roman blind.

▷ ▽ *Growing points*

Progressing to a totally adult and sophisticated living room can take quite a while – and careful planning. Stage 2 (right) retains a practical family eating area and easily vacuumed wall-to-wall carpeting. The new sofa and chair are upholstered in a hard-wearing weave. Scatter cushions tie in the new acquisitions with the existing curtains. Stylish modern nesting tables replace a previous coffee table – and provide more resting places, too.

The move to Stage 3 (below) seems like quite a jump, but there are links with the room's past. The same dining table is still in use, completely hidden by an extravagant swathe of cream chintz. The apricot tones of Stage 2 have moved to the windows, which are dressed with sheer austrian blinds and translucent curtains that echo the rich pattern on the upholstered chairs. There's plenty of wood in evidence – from the rich hardwood floor to smart display units. A new cornice reinforces the richness. The overall result is warm, chic and very sophisticated.

Cool breeze A fan such as the one shown serves two purposes. Set high from the ceiling, it circulates air throughout the room, cooling the room in summer and pushing warm air down in winter. Also, as many fans come equipped with lights, it can add to the lighting scheme.

TRICKS AND TREATS

There are several simple 'tricks of the trade' that can help you make the transition through the various stages. Use paint to link diverse pieces of furniture together – either as solid color or, more subtly, marbled or sponged in two or three different shades. Alternatively, you could stencil a design in one or two corners of a chest, a cabinet door, or an old table. Paint techniques work equally well on small accessories, too.

A serviceable but unexciting carpet – or perhaps one that's worn in a few places – will be enhanced if you treat yourself to the best rug you can afford and let its colors lead naturally into the next stage of your room scheme.

If you'd like elaborately dressed curtains but find that you can't afford the real thing, look out for inexpensive fabrics such as muslin or curtain lining. Seconds or ends of rolls of voiles or light cottons are other budget buys well worth considering. Drape generous quantities of the low-cost fabric you have chosen over a pole, using Velcro to hold it in place.

Give worn furniture new life by throwing a length of coordinating fabric over it – perhaps an Indian-style cloth or even a soft rug. These measures all help to create a comfortable room to live in while you progress through different stages.

△ *Marbling style*
Maximum coordination can be achieved at minimum cost by employing a special paint technique. Here, marbling has been used on everything from the mantel to the picture frames, subtly enhancing the wallcovering.

▽ *Paint extras*
Delicate paint work enhances a lavender-and-neutral color scheme. Note the trompe l'oeil fireplace with color-washed mantel. The walls are decorated with painted dots and a carefully stenciled border.

SEATING ARRANGEMENTS

The sitting area forms the heart of any living room and requires careful planning to make it work successfully.

The seating in a living room needs to be comfortable and flexible, so that it can be rearranged to suit a variety of activities. In winter it is cozier to face into the room – perhaps towards a blazing fire. In summer you'll probably want to make the most of the light and the view outside the window.

Conversation circle A group of people naturally form themselves into a circle around a focal point such as a fireplace and/or a coffee table.

This circle must be self-contained and should not be crossed by others passing through to reach the kitchen or the hall, for instance. If the living room contains a dining section, the ideal is to keep the two areas separate and well-defined.

In addition to the main seating area, an isolated corner where one or two people can talk or read away from the main group works well, especially in a large household.

Furniture Sofas and chairs are the most noticeable pieces of furniture in a living room. They affect the character of the room and the mood you wish to create.

Scale is an important consideration. Giant sofas look wonderful in big rooms but you'll be forever climbing over them in small ones. Likewise, dainty furniture can easily look lost in a very spacious room.

The shape of the room will have a bearing on whether you can achieve the exact arrangement you want. Make the best possible use of the space in which you have to work; you may be able to turn an apparent disadvantage into an asset.

A long narrow room, for example, often ends up with a wasted area at one end. It is better to create two, separate, intimate groups of seating, each for four people, than to have a large, spread-out arrangement.

Three-piece classic
With no fireplace in this room it is easier to rearrange the three-piece set. The sofa could face the view with a chair on either side.

SEATING ARRANGEMENTS

The three-piece set was the most popular combination of living room furniture for many years; it was almost impossible to buy sofas and chairs separately. But nowadays you don't have to have a three-seater sofa and two matching armchairs unless you really choose to.

The problem with such a set is that it is not very flexible. The logical way to place the pieces is with the sofa in the center and a chair on either side. And although the sofa is called a three-seater, three people sitting in a row is not ideal for conversation.

An arrangement of two roomy, two-seater sofas plus an armchair provides the same number of places but is much more versatile. The two sofas can face each other, or they can work equally well placed at right angles to each other. The armchair can be moved into or out of the circle as required.

Other flexible alternatives are three chairs and a two-seater sofa; or a group of four or five armchairs. If you decide on the latter, be careful with your choice of shapes or you could get a broken up effect. One way to avoid this is to have at least two chairs in matching fabric.

A chaise longue is a wonderful indulgence if you have the space. To achieve a similar effect, choose a chair with a matching footstool.

Coverings Whatever arrangement you opt for, you don't need to have all your seating covered with the same fabric. It is more chic to mix plains with a pattern or patterns of different scales or closely related colors.

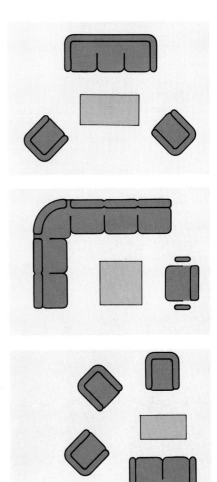

△ **Seating circles** Top to bottom:
□ A three-seater sofa and two armchairs are a traditional choice.
□ Add a chair to unit seating to complete the circle.
□ A two-seater plus three chairs is a flexible choice.

△ **Convivial plan**
Two sofas placed one on either side of a fireplace is a good layout for conversation. A table between them is useful for coffee or drinks and helps to 'anchor' the seating.

◁ **Ringing the changes**
An alternative set-up for the same room has two sofas at right angles to each other, plus an armchair.

▷ **Tailored look**
A three-seater and small two-seater are a neat option in a small room. The clean geometric lines of the seating are echoed by the rectangular rug and square coffee table; a glass-topped table appears to take up less of the floor space than a solid one.

OTHER CHOICES

Living room seating does not have to consist entirely of conventional sofas and armchairs.

Informal style You may prefer to mix a traditional sofa with less formal wicker chairs, giving a less crowded look to a small room. Another option is a fully upholstered sofa and chair plus a chair with a wooden frame. In either case, you should give the pieces a sense of unity by linking them via the patterns or colors used in the covering.

Modern setting Modular seating made up of some armless chairs and corner units can be used to fit a larger number of people into an area than could be accommodated more conventionally.

Units can be put together to make an L- or U-shape, depending on the space available. In many ranges the corner unit can be replaced by a small table. A right or left arm can usually be used appropriately to end a run. This kind of seating works well combined with one or two chairs that can be drawn up to complete the circle when needed.

△ *Conservatory mood*
A sofa and two wicker chairs give a less crowded look to a room that also has to house a piano. The same summery fabric is used on all seating; the theme is carried through with pale walls and plants.

▽ *Spacious attic*
Modular units make a neat L-shape in this attic and, with an extra chair, are a good layout for conversation. The uncluttered feel is enhanced by keeping everything pale except the seating, which is in strong grays.

COMFORTABLE SEATING

Take the time to plan seating to suit your needs, your home and lifestyle.

Comfortable seating for reading, watching television, listening to music, knitting, sewing, eating or simply relaxing is the first big furniture buy most home-owners make. Seating is so important to comfortable living that it is worth buying the very best you can afford. It pays to take the time to make sure the furniture suits your needs and is a pleasure to use.

MAKE A ROOM PLAN

Once you have assessed your needs, make a plan of the room in which you are going to use the furniture. This seems unnecessarily fussy but is well worthwhile. Sofas and chairs may look a reasonable size in a large furniture showroom, but can be much too large for a domestic living or dining room.

The basic plan Draw the shape of the room on graph paper, allowing one square per ½in. Mark windows, doors, and permanent objects in color. Draw the shapes of existing furniture that is going to remain in the room on graph paper, using the same scale as the main plan, and cut them out. If you have an existing dining table but want to buy new chairs, measure the space from the underside of the table edge to the floor and mark it on your plan. This helps you to choose chairs to fit comfortably under the table.

First steps Armed with your checklist, go through manufacturers' brochures and cut out chairs and sofas you like the look of and which suit your needs. Draw the shapes on graph paper, using manufacturers' measurements as a guide. Cut the shapes out and color them in so that they stand out from the main room plan. Write the name of the model on the back of each piece.

Traffic flow Take into account the traffic flow through the room when arranging furniture pieces on your plan. Lightly mark in the flow patterns from one door to another to make sure that seating won't cross any of the main pathways through the room. In a small or awkwardly shaped room, sectional seating, where pieces can be pushed together or separated as needed, are probably more flexible than two sofas or a sofa and two chairs. Folding chairs are extremely useful in a small room.

Space Remember to allow enough space in front of furniture for people to stand up and sit down easily. It is important to allow a minimum of 24in. for someone to walk into or around a room without having to squeeze past furniture. When dining chairs are grouped around a table, each chair needs 5-6in. of space on either side to allow diners to get in and out easily, and to eat without bumping elbows.

ASSESS YOUR NEEDS

Before you buy seating, sit down and assess your needs, using the checklist shown here.

Who will use the seating?
- ☐ Children
- ☐ Adults
- ☐ Elderly people

If an elderly person uses the room on a regular basis, you need a chair designed to suit his or her needs. If children and pets use the room, you need washable, hard-wearing upholstery.

How many people use the room regularly?
- ☐ 2-4
- ☐ 4-6
- ☐ 6-8

How do they use the room?
- ☐ Watching TV
- ☐ Homework
- ☐ Reading
- ☐ Hobbies
- ☐ Play
- ☐ Eating
- ☐ Listening to music

Think about the selection of chairs needed for these activities. Two recliners mounted on a swivel base might, for instance, be more useful than two armchairs when one person wants to read or listen to music (using headphones) and the other wants to watch television.

Will extra seating be needed?
- ☐ Not often
- ☐ Often (weekly)

Consider flexible unit seating if you regularly need extra chairs.

RELAXING SEATING

Your assessment and plan show what type of seating to look for but it is only by sitting in a chair that you can find out whether or not it is comfortable. Upholstered relaxing seating can be a combination of chairs and sofas, two or more sofas, or unit furniture that can be pushed together to make sofas or separated into chairs as needed. There are several important characteristics that affect the comfort of seating.

Seat slope The seat should slope slightly from front to back so that your body is in a relaxed position. Avoid seating with a pronounced slope – it curves the spine at an angle that is too acute for comfort.

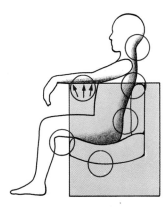

△ **The wrong chair**
This chair has no support for the head, neck or spine. The seat is too low and the arms too high.

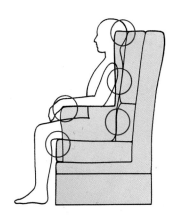

△ **The right chair**
A high back supports the head, neck and spine. The arms and seat are the right height for relaxation.

Seat height The front part of the seat should be at a height that does not apply pressure to the back of your legs. If there is an adult in the family above or below average height, look for a chair a little higher or lower to suit them. Avoid very low chairs or sofas that apply pressure to the back of the legs and are difficult to get in and out of. An elderly or disabled person needs a chair with a fairly high seat for ease of movement.

Seat width The seat should be wide enough to allow freedom of movement. If your legs or ribs press against the sides of the seat, it is too narrow.

Softness A very soft chair may seem appealing but isn't as comfortable to sit in long-term as a well-sprung seat that supports your body. Quality springs usually equal a high price but are worthwhile as cushions keep their shape (cheap cushions stuffed with foam chips compress at the front, go lumpy and become uncomfortable) and the chair is more resistant to hard wear.

Back height Low-backed seating where support ends below shoulder level is very uncomfortable. If you want low-backed seating, look for a design where the back reaches shoulder height. High-backed seating gives extra support to the back as well as your neck and shoulders. Head rests add to comfort but should be adjustable. Thick, fixed head-rests are often positioned so that the center of the head is supported but the neck isn't, which can be uncomfortable.

Arms Chair and sofa arms should be wide enough and at the right height for you to rest your arms in comfort.

▽ *For the elderly*
This chair is the perfect shape for an elderly person. It has a high seat and back with a headrest.

▽ *Stressless seating*
The ultimate relaxer reclines with you, has an adjustable headrest, swivels with a smooth action and offers a comfortable footstool.

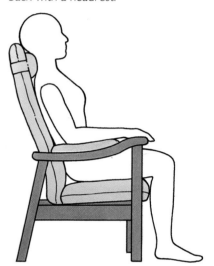

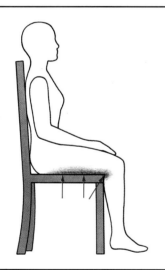

◁ *Pressure points*
A dining chair that is too high will press uncomfortably against the back of your knees and thighs.

EATING CHAIRS
Dining chairs must be considered with the dining table. If you are buying chairs to match an existing table, remember to take the measurements for the size of the table and its height from the floor with you. If you are buying a new table and chairs, try the two together.

Height If a dining chair is too high, your legs tend to press against both the underside of the table and the front edge of the chair. If it is too low, eating is difficult. A gap of about 12in. between the top of the table and your knees is right for most adults.

Arms The arms on carver chairs should be at the right height to rest elbows in comfort. Seat width is important on dining chairs with arms – if the seat is too narrow, the arms will press against the ribs and thighs of the person sitting in the chair.

Back height Look for chairs that give support up to shoulder level. Stooping over food gives most people indigestion, so avoid very low-backed dining chairs that encourage this.

WORKING CHAIRS
An upright dining chair is not suitable for use during long periods of study or typing. If a member of your family works at home on a regular basis, it is worth buying a special typist's chair or a Scandinavian posture chair designed to hold the spine in the right position. Sitting on the wrong type of chair to use a keyboard can lead to backache.

▷ *Working comfortably*
This is the wrong chair for a typist as it offers no back support and slopes badly.

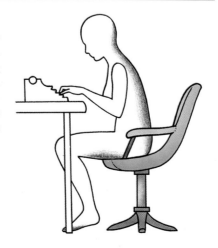

SEATING FOR THE ELDERLY
When buying seating for an elderly person, look for the following:

Seat height The seat should be high enough to allow the user to get in and out of the chair easily.

Back height Most older people find a high-backed chair comfortable.

Seat slope Don't buy a chair that slopes acutely – an old person may find it difficult to get in and out of.

CHOOSING A SOFA

Buying a sofa is a major investment so it pays to consider the options carefully.

There's a strong trend today towards having one or two sofas and a few occasional chairs instead of the traditional three-piece set. If your living room can accommodate two sofas there are many design options. The sofas can be identical – a classic approach – or different – a more adventurous choice.

Either way, sofas are major investments, and you should know what is available before making your choice. Seating capacity, versatility, practicality, style and cost are all considerations. A compromise is usually necessary and it should be the best possible for you.

Size and style The terms 'two' and 'three' seater are misleading: most two seaters only take two tightly fitted adults. For comfort, two people need a three seater. Make sure that a large three seater really does seat three adults comfortably.

Consider external dimensions in relation to room size as well as internal ones such as seat height and depth, back height and length. Bear in mind that:
□ low seats are difficult for older people to get up from,
□ tall people with long legs need a deeper seat,
□ very soft sofas don't support you properly,
□ a low back will not support your head and shoulders,
□ the arm rests should be at a comfortable height.

The style you choose can complement an existing scheme: a Victorian-type chesterfield in a Victorian-style living room is a safe bet. A sofa's style can also contrast with its surroundings: the same chesterfield can look superb in a stark modern room. There are also many timeless styles that are 'at home' in a wide range of schemes.

Comfort and cost A sofa is a major purchase so don't rush into it. To a certain extent you get what you pay for. The price is likely to reflect both the construction – a really comfortable spring system – and the quality of the covering fabric. Bear in mind that an upholstered sofa is usually covered in the fabric of your choice, so it will take at least 8-18

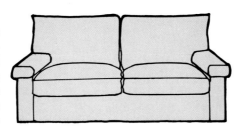

△ LOW-ARMED TWO SEATER
Style Its simple modern shape can also be used in any sort of scheme.
In use Though compact, the low arms make the sofa easier for lounging in than the love seat.
Watchpoint Check on quality of upholstery. Cheap foam can easily lose its shape.

△ BAMBOO SOFA
Style A light-looking sofa for sun rooms, Oriental or conservatory-style rooms.
In use The bamboo frame may not stand up to long, hard wear.
Watchpoint Cushions must be well filled, as the frame is not upholstered. Covers should unzip for easy cleaning.

▽ HIGH-BACKED THREE SEATER
Style An old-fashioned sofa with the emphasis on comfort.
In use A good lounging, relaxing sofa. Can be covered in any fabric, patterned or plain.
Watchpoint Can be oppressive as part of a three-piece set, especially in a small room.

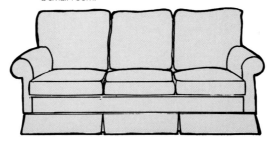

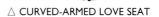

△ CURVED-ARMED LOVE SEAT
Style This shape fits well into any traditional or modern scheme.
In use Good for small rooms or as an extra sofa, but it only seats two at close quarters – hence the term love seat – and it is not good for 'sprawlers.'
Watchpoint Arms get dirty quickly: choose dark or patterned covers, or a light fabric that has been treated.

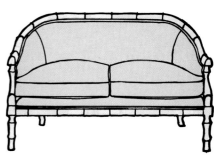

△ WOOD-FRAMED SOFA
Style Elegantly traditional, good in a classically decorated room or large bedroom.
In use Not for lounging. This is definitely formal seating.
Watchpoint Plain or small-scale geometric print fabric, such as velvet or damask, is in keeping with its formal shape. Avoid chintz.

△ CURVED THREE SEATER
Style Traditional, comfortable and plump.
In use The informal, curved shape makes it easy for three people to sit and converse.
Watchpoint Upholstered base could get dirty quickly. Avoid light fabrics unless treated. Not suitable for loose covers.

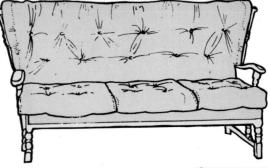

weeks to deliver. (The chapter on upholstered furniture on pages 55-56 gives more information on sofa construction and upholstery fabrics.)

Even on a tight budget, you are better off buying a quality sofa covered with a second-rate fabric, than buying a sofa that has a frame that will not withstand the test of time. A washable loose cover should be sufficient until you can replace it with a more luxurious fabric.

◁ 'SETTLE' HIGH-BACK
Style Definitely traditional.
In use High back and curved sides make this ideal for a drafty room. Not for sprawling or lounging; good as an extra sofa.
Watchpoint The frame should be steady enough to support the top-heavy structure.

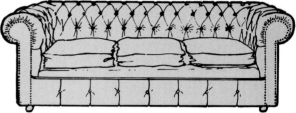

△ CHESTERFIELD
Style This design fits into both traditional and contemporary schemes. Leather-covered versions are particularly versatile, though expensive.
In use Comfortable both to sit and lounge on, and worth considering for the 'one-sofa' room.
Watchpoint If 'button-back,' buttons should be securely attached. Loose covers spoil the line.

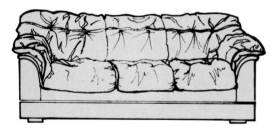

△ MODERN COUCH
Style Generally leather covered, this shaped sofa is definitely for a modern room.
In use Suitable for informal sprawling and lounging.
Watchpoint Not good for back problems, as there is minimal support. Check that buttons are firmly sewn.

▽ CAMEL-BACKED THREE SEATER
Style Definitely traditional.
In use As good for curling up in as for stretching out.
Watchpoint Can dominate a small room, and often better on its own than as part of a three-piece set.

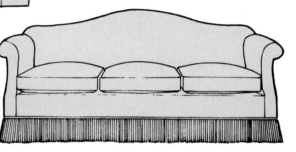

▽ TUBULAR TWO SEATER
Style Modern enough for a contemporary setting, though would provide a note of contrast in a traditional scheme.
In use Adequate seating but not especially comfortable. Usually covered in plain fabric or leather.
Watchpoint Check cushion filling: lumps and bumps spoil the line.

◁ DUVET SOFA
Style A leather- or fabric-covered bag with a soft filling is draped over a firm base and attached on the underside. Suits modern and uncluttered rooms.
In use Leather-covered sofas 'mature' with age and acquire an attractive patina.
Watchpoint Make sure the base is firm enough and a good support.

▷ ARMLESS COUCH
Style Modern seating for a modern room.
In use Great for lounging, but no corners to curl up in. Usually upholstered in a plain fabric.
Watchpoint Unsuitable for loose covers. Get extra fabric for a few scatter cushions, if possible.

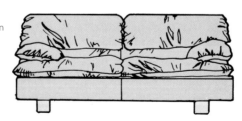

▽ MODULAR UNIT SEATING
Style Best for large-scale modern rooms.
In use Theoretically, modular seating offers maximum flexibility, as seats can either be pushed together or used separately.
Watchpoint Can look somewhat impersonal in large doses. Not very comfortable if armless, awkward to use separately if one-armed.

◁ SQUARED-UP LOVE SEAT
Style Good for small rooms, modern or traditional, or as second sofa. Good, also, in pairs.
In use For sitting only. More comfortable for one person than for two.
Watchpoint Tight-fitting cushions essential.

CHOOSING AN ARMCHAIR

Choose an armchair to suit your room and your needs – something to curl up in or give your back support.

The traditional three-piece set consists of a sofa and two matching armchairs. Today, living room furniture is much more flexible and you can have a variety of seating options depending on the size of your room and the style of the furnishings.

The sofa and armchair don't have to be the same style or even be covered in the same fabric, so you can buy them at different times.

Most of the considerations outlined in Choosing a Sofa, on the previous two pages, apply to armchairs too. Cost is usually directly related to the type of construction used and the quality of the fabric covering. If you spend more on the construction and less on the fabric the chair will last longer, and you can always re-cover it later in a better fabric when funds permit. When you choose the fabric for upholstery, buy enough to make up arm and head covers that can be removed for cleaning as these areas get dirty and worn first.

There is no substitute for actually sitting in the chair itself for a reasonable length of time to find out if it suits you. If support for your head and shoulders is important avoid low-backed-chairs but make sure that the back is at the right height for you and does not push your head forward. Arms should be positioned so that yours rest comfortably and the seat should not be so low that getting up is difficult.

TRADITIONAL ARMCHAIR STYLES

CURVED TUB
Style The arms curve around and up to form the back. Lightweight versions have show wood legs and no seat cushion; more solid versions have an upholstered or valanced base with a fitted seat cushion.
In use Ideal for additional seating or in a room where space is limited.
Watchpoint The low back does not give much support.

CHESTERFIELD
Style Essentially a miniature version of the chesterfield sofa - medium height with deep buttoning and solid arms. Upholstered in fabric or leather.
In use High arms restrict sprawling but make a cozy corner to curl up in.
Watchpoint They take up a lot of room – check external measurements – and the style can look heavy unless there is plenty of space. Loose covers spoil the line.

WING BACK
Style This traditional high-backed style with scroll arms has carved cabriole front legs. Variations in the design include a buttoned back and a slightly less padded version with show wood arm supports, and straight front legs. Available upholstered in both fabric and leather.
In use Most models are lightweight, both to move around and to look at. The high back provides support to back and head and is ideal for use in a drafty room.
Watchpoints Firmly upholstered over a rigid frame, this is not a chair to lounge in. Not all shapes are suitable for loose covers although the seat cushion cover may be removable. If button backed, pull on the buttons to check they are sewn on firmly.

BEDROOM CHAIR
Style Small low chair without arms. The high back can be curved or straight, buttoned or plain, with an attractively shaped top edge.
In use Originally designed for bedrooms but ideal as additional seating particularly in a small living room.

HIGH-BACK SCROLL ARM
Style A high-backed chair with scroll arms angled outwards and a generous seat.
In use A cushion or two adds comfort to the deep square seat. Suitable for fitted loose covers.
Watchpoint A solid piece of furniture that takes up space and looks as though it does.

CURVED ARM
Style An elegant chair with tapering arms that curve outwards, and shaped-back and deep seat cushions.
In use The formal style looks good in modern and traditional rooms.
Watchpoint Check the covers are removable for cleaning.

CURVED BACK
Style A traditional design with generous curves and a deep comfy seat.
In use The curved back looks softer than square backed versions.
Watchpoint Not very good for posture – the low back encourages sprawling.

MODERN STYLES

SQUARED UP

Style A low-backed chair with high slim arms and a square seat cushion. Neat and compact, it suits both modern and traditional rooms.

In use Like the chesterfield this square shape is not suitable for sprawling but makes a comfy seat. The cover is loose for easy cleaning.

Watchpoint Check that there is sufficient density of foam covering the wooden frame.

BAMBOO

Style A lightweight bamboo frame (usually made from steamed beech and treated to look like bamboo) holds deep comfy cushions. Styles include many classic armchair shapes including the squared-up and tub.

In use Ideal for conservatory or Oriental-style rooms.

Watchpoint Not so strong or long lasting as chairs with a conventional solid construction.

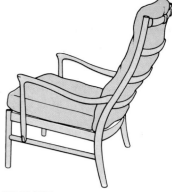

WOOD FRAME

Style These lightweight chairs are not upholstered, simply a show wood frame supporting a pair of covered cushions. Suit a country-style room.

In use Not chairs for lounging in, but the firm back gives good support. The back can be high or low and a rocking-chair version is also available.

Watchpoint Check the density of the cushions and make sure the frame joints are strong.

SWIVEL RECLINER

Style Modern in style and made from chrome and upholstered in leather or fabric. Usually on a pedestal base, this office chair is often now seen in the home.

In use Can be adjusted to any angle right to the horizontal. Some designs also have an extending leg rest.

Watchpoint Expensive.

LEATHER AND CHROME

Style Definitely for a modern room style. A variety of designs – the seat and back can be upholstered or simply leather slung across the frame something like a deck chair.

In use Not a lounging chair but lightweight to look at and to move around.

Watchpoint Leather wears in beautifully but greasy marks and scratches are impossible to remove.

SQUARE LOW ARMED

Style A high-backed chair with feather or foam-filled cushions and broad comfy arms. Suitable for most traditionally furnished rooms.

In use The low arms make this an ideal chair for lounging. The seat and back cushion covers can be removed for cleaning.

Watchpoint Check the density of the foam covering the frame.

ARMLESS MODERN

Style Usually covered in leather or a heavy textured plain fabric. Some styles look as though an upholstered duvet has been draped over the frame. Most suitable for a modern style of furnishing.

In use An informal chair that encourages sprawling.

Watchpoint Little support for backs.

MODULAR UNITS

Style Fabric-covered sculptured foam blocks. Look for corner units, and end units with arms, for versatility.

In use Can be put together to form a run or fit into awkward space. Relatively cheap to buy and the covers are removable for easy cleaning.

Watchpoint Low backs mean little support for head and shoulders and encourage lounging. Not very comfortable if armless and difficult to use separately if one armed

BEAN BAG

Style Colorful canvas or leather bags filled with polystyrene granules.

In use Versatile additional seating, ideal for a first home or children's rooms.

Watchpoint Check whether the granules are in a lining bag that is easy to remove when washing the outer cover. The granules will compact in time and may need fluffing up

UPHOLSTERED FURNITURE

When buying upholstered furniture, looks, durability and comfort are key points to remember.

Upholstered furniture is expensive but it is one of those areas where you definitely get what you pay for. Cheap furniture won't last long and it won't keep its looks – some can appear old after only a few weeks of use. And make no mistake, upholstered furniture is subjected to much harder wear than cupboards, tables and other furniture. So it needs to be of sufficient quality to withstand repeated movement and weight, as well as look good.

Secondhand upholstered furniture may be a good short term buy if it is in reasonable condition. Bear in mind that if you have to have it reupholstered or re-covered professionally it may end up costing as much as buying new. Sales are good places to buy upholstered furniture, but do some careful research and don't be taken in by an apparent bargain.

The style of the sofa or seat should suit those people who will be sitting on it; tall people are generally more comfortable in high-backed seats, short people in low, shallow seats so their feet can reach the floor, while the elderly and very young find low seating difficult to get out of.

Follow the checklist suggested below before parting with your money.

WOOD FRAME SOFA

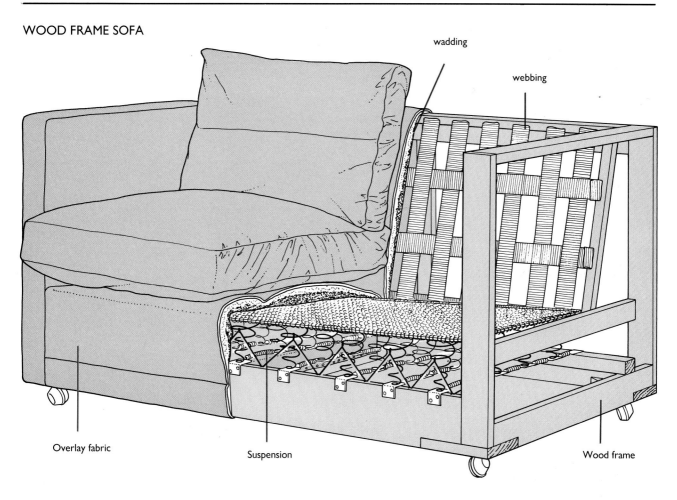

wadding

webbing

Overlay fabric

Suspension

Wood frame

FRAMES

Chair and sofa frames are made of wood, metal or plastic. Provided they are good quality and put together well, each of these materials will do a good job.

Wood frames may be hardwood or softwood. Hardwood frames are better for furniture where the wood shows. Softwood tends to dent and scratch easily and can soon start to look worn. But where the wood is not on show softwood makes a satisfactory frame and is cheaper than hardwood.

Traditionally, wooden frames were fixed together with dowels – circular wooden pegs – and these are still found on high-quality furniture.

But good quality frames may also be put together with screws or staples used with glue. It is always worth asking the salesperson if they have a cutaway version of what you are buying.

The illustration shows a cutaway view of a good quality sofa construction. The hardwood frame is doweled, glued and screwed together before being covered with coil springing; this is then held in place by ties. Each layer of padding over the springs makes the piece of furniture more comfortable. Here, the springs are covered with hessian, a coir fiber pad, two layers of cotton felt and a calico outer layer. It is now ready to be covered in fabric.

55

Metal frames can be the external supporting framework (often chrome finished as shown), which add to the overall appearance of the piece, or – like wood – they can form an integral but concealed part of the piece of furniture. Those built on the lines of deck chairs tend to be less robust than the more traditional styles and are not a good choice if wear is likely to be hard.

Plastic frames are molded to a specific shape and may then have an upholstered seat and/or back. It would be to your advantage if a completely upholstered piece has a plastic frame because it will be lighter than one with a wooden or metal frame. However, some plastic frames are sometimes weighted to keep them steady and prevent them from tipping over. Unweighted plastic furniture can be an advantage in rooms where you need to be able to move furniture around easily.

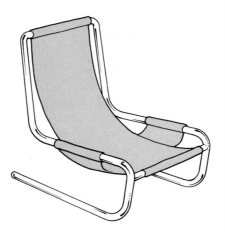

FRAME CHECKPOINTS
☐ Look at as much of the frame as you can see. Check wood for knots, cracks and poor finish.
☐ Joints should be firmly fixed and all traces of loose bits of glue should be wiped away.
☐ Corner supports for legs should be sound as they have to take strain, especially back legs on upright chairs.
☐ Move the furniture to see if the casters run smoothly.
☐ Lean the arms back and outwards to make sure they don't have too much give.

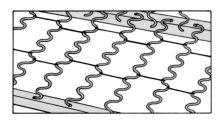
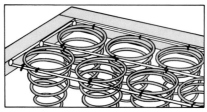
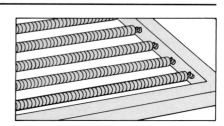

SUSPENSION
The suspension is the part of the chair or sofa that supports the seating and seat back. The most common structure in well-made upholstered furniture is vertically positioned coil springing supported on webbing. Webbing is the name given to a latticework of supports made, for example, from fabric or rubber, which runs between the seat and back frame. Alternatively, this is replaced by horizontally linked tension springing.

SUSPENSION CHECKPOINTS
☐ Sit on the piece to check that there are no individual springs sticking up.

☐ Rock from side to side on the seat to see that webbing is stretched evenly.

☐ Springs or webbing should be well fixed and not rubbing against anything.

☐ When you get up from the seat make sure that it resumes its shape quickly.

☐ Look for a seat that is harder than the back of the chair. The seat takes more weight and daily wear and tear so it should be much stronger.

FILLINGS
Some of the more expensive upholstered furniture is still filled with traditional materials such as horse hair and cotton flock, but most modern pieces are upholstered with plastic or polyfoam. It is difficult to judge foam quality in a shop but it is very important that it is of a high density. Question the sales assistant about this. Low-grade foam does not hold its shape and disintegrates quickly. Feel the foam for thickness and firmness and sit on it to check both properties.

Dome-shaped seat cushions indicate firm supportive filling. If cushions are feather-filled make sure there are no sharp quills protruding through the covering fabric and that movement and weight on the cushions do not alter their shape too much.

FILLING CHECKPOINTS
☐ Sit on the piece to check it for comfort and support, and watch how quickly the cushions spring back into shape.
☐ Look for a dome-shaped seat. Foam, whatever the quality, will settle and flatten out with use.
☐ Be sure to buy furniture that has passed fire resistance tests. Those that have passed are marked with a special tag.

COVERS
When buying a piece of furniture, consider how you are going to clean it. Tightly covered furniture requires an upholstery shampoo or a visit from a professional cleaner. Loose covers can be removed for washing or dry cleaning. The entire sofa need not be cleaned – often, simply cleaning removable seat covers, which tend to receive the most wear, makes all the difference.

A pair of arm caps reduces wear on a piece of furniture's arms. If these are not supplied ready-made with the furniture or cannot be ordered, try to obtain a length of matching fabric and make or have them made yourself.

High-backed chairs may become dirty where heads rest. It is a good idea to try to get some extra fabric to make matching back covers that can be washed or dry-cleaned separately.

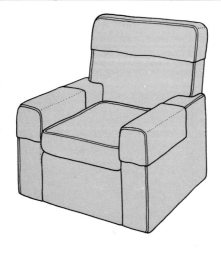

COVER CHECKPOINTS
☐ Overlocked seams won't fray.
☐ Reversible cushions last longer than those that can be used on only one side, provided you turn them regularly.
☐ Piping on the front of seat cushions or on arm edges will wear with constant rubbing.
☐ Check fabric for flaws.
☐ Make sure buttons on furniture are fixed securely.
☐ If the service is available, order extra covers for the arms and head. This will extend the life of the cover.
☐ Pale-colored plain fabrics tend to reveal dirt and grime.

TRADITIONAL OCCASIONAL TABLES

The classic designs of period furniture are the inspiration for many of today's traditional-style occasional tables.

Much of today's occasional table furniture derives from classic period furniture designs, usually adapted to machine production methods and adjusted to suit present-day living. Height, for instance, may be altered when copying an original or the size may be scaled down.

Uses Many period-style occasional tables these days are put to very different uses from those for which they were designed. (Most were originally intended for use in houses where furniture was often more decorative than functional.) This is one of the reasons why reproductions are seldom exact – the style is copied but sizes are adapted to fit in with today's needs.

Influences and inspiration Many reproductions are inspired by furniture from the Georgian period – the early 18th century to early 19th century. The latter part is generally termed Regency and the period is pre-dated by Queen Anne and the Stuart and Tudor periods.

The outstanding makers and designers of the time were William Kent, Thomas Chippendale, Robert Adam, George Hepplewhite, Thomas Hope and Thomas Sheraton, among others. These names are often found associated with reproduction furniture but very little is an exact copy of an original design or even made in the same way.

Another strong influence are the many rustic designs and pieces from Victorian country pine furniture, which are not classed as 'fine' furniture, but nevertheless have a solid, homey charm. Indeed you may be able to find original pieces at reasonable prices quite easily. This kind of furniture, although fashionable, does not command nearly the same price premium as fine antique furniture – that is, furniture made before about 1830.

Materials All period-style occasional furniture is made either from solid or veneered wood, perhaps with a leather or glass top if appropriate. The most commonly found woods are mahogany, walnut and cherry or other fruitwood for traditional styles, while oak and pine are the most usual for rustic styles.

Illustrated below are examples of the many occasional tables in period styles that are reproduced and available in today's stores. (For an explanation of some of the terms used, refer to Glossary of Terms next page.)

COFFEE TABLES

In use This category is made up of a mixture of period-style tables that could be used as coffee tables even though they weren't necessarily designed for this purpose. The height and size of table that you choose depends on the size of your sofa and chairs. (If you intend using the table for TV meals, be sure it is high enough.)

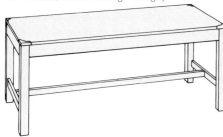

18TH-CENTURY STYLE
Style Twin tripod pedestals with crossbanded edging give this piece a very elegant look.

LOW CIRCULAR
Style This low circular table makes a good sized coffee table. It has a four splay pedestal base with classic lion's head casters.
Watchpoint Takes up a deceptive amount of space.

MILITARY STYLE
Style Typified by plain construction and brass corners. This makes a strong, robust table that could fit into most house surroundings.

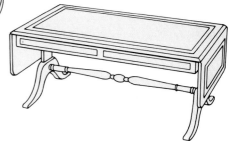

LONG JOHN
Style The shape of this type of coffee table explains its name. It is a popular and practical shape reproduced in many different styles. This lyre-ended type with rounded top and twin-turned stretchers is based on a traditional style.

SOFA TABLE
Style A sofa table is generally higher than most coffee tables, but more often than not, serves the same purpose. This Regency-style table has an extendable drop-end. Originally it would have been drawn up to the sofa for two people to sit at while drinking or playing a parlor game.

COCKTAIL TABLE
Style Introduced in the 1920s when cocktails first became popular, this style of cocktail table has drop-end supports taken from Regency styles, with turned stretcher and skivered top.

SMALL TABLES

In use This type of table is likely to be used for decorative rather than purely practical purposes. Wine tables, for example, were intended to be used to serve wine, but are excellent display units for potted plants, china, photos, and so on. The less-delicately proportioned drum tables can take a single, striking object.

WINE TABLE

Style Usually found with a tripod base and a central column. They often have a pie crust rim around the top which prevents glasses from being knocked off. This one has a cluster column on a tripod base.

DRUM TABLE

Style Circular Regency-style drum table on turned pedestal with tripod legs on casters. These were mostly used as game/card tables. Drawer fronts are usually mock, although sometimes there is a shelf below the drum top for magazines.

NESTING TABLES

Style Nests of tables, as the name implies, nest one inside the other and are therefore very

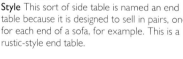

space saving. They can also make an attractive feature in a room.

Sheraton-style nesting tables (above left) nest conventionally one inside the other. Rustic-style,

nesting tables (above right) are sturdy and chunky with scalloped under edge. The two identical smaller-tables nest side by side under the large table.

SIDE TABLES

In use The two main kinds of side table generally used to flank a sofa, are either called end or lamp tables. (There is little difference between the two.) A console or hall table, designed to stand against a wall in the hallway, is also a type of side table.

HALL/CONSOLE TABLE

Style Elegant form of side table designed originally for the hallway or reception room wall – very often accompanied by a matching wall mirror. The narrow, tapered legs are typical of the 1700s.

END TABLE

Style This sort of side table is named an end table because it is designed to sell in pairs, one for each end of a sofa, for example. This is a rustic-style end table.

LAMP TABLE

Style Square table with apron base and four slender turned columns that end in ball finials. Specifically made to hold table lamps, this type of table often has a lip/rim around the top as a safeguard. Drawers are for magazines and so on.

GLOSSARY OF TERMS

Apron base Shaped piece below table base.

Cluster column Thin, turned vertical supports grouped in threes to form single columns.

Cross banding Contrasting wooden or veneer strip bordering the edge of drawer front or table top at right angles to main grain.

Drop-end Hinged extension flat on an end (or both ends) of a table.

Finials Ornamental spikes, balls or other shapes projecting upward, usually from top corners.

Lyre-end A table leg shaped like the musical instrument, the lyre.

Pedestal Central supporting column.

Pie crust Carved raised rim.

Skivered Leather-topped, usually gold, green or red.

Splay Turned out at an angle.

Stretcher Strengthening link between legs.

Turning Decorative shaping done on a lathe (hence turned legs).

MODERN OCCASIONAL TABLES

One or two occasional tables in a living room are handy and practical pieces of furniture for everyday use.

Modern occasional tables can be loosely divided into five main categories: coffee tables, nests of tables, magazine and storage tables, sofa/lamp tables and console or side tables. However, within these categories there is a wide variety of shapes, styles and sizes, making modern occasional tables far more flexible than period-style pieces.

MATERIALS
While period-style occasional tables are made of a relatively limited selection of materials the choice for modern tables is wide.

Wood Wooden tables may be made of solid or veneered wood (see page 67). Mahogany, teak and rosewood are commonly found; ash is often stained or lacquered in black or charcoal, and a light stone 'limed' finish is popular on oak and ash.

Tabletops may be plain or decorative wood, glass or tiled. Glass and tiled tops have the great advantage of being relatively tough and easy to clean. However, if you have children in the house, it is important to check that the glass complies with safety standards.

Lacquer Lacquer finishes range from a light coating that allows the wood grain to show, to a solid glossy coat of dense color, usually white, cream, gray or black. The effect can be plain or very glitzy when combined with brass, chrome, glass or rigid plastic.

Rattan and cane Rattan furniture is sometimes wrongly called bamboo, which is much thinner, but it may include bamboo or cane weaving. As well as its natural coloring, rattan and cane furniture may be colored – black or white is most often found – but it is available in a wide range of colors. Tops are often glass.

Chipboard Circular chipboard tables are designed to be covered with a floor-length cloth. They are very economical to buy and, if you use them with a protective glass top, very practical.

Others You may come across polished granite tops, marble or onyx tables, perhaps topped with glass. These are extremely durable and virtually indestructible, but they are expensive, so should be bought only if they are going to fit in with the long term plans of your room schemes.

Chrome, laminate, glass and rigid plastic are common. Bear in mind that rigid plastic is unlikely to last a long time.

Modular table units designed to match seating units are upholstered in the same fabric as the seating and usually have an inset glass or wooden top. They are most often used to form the link in a corner seating arrangement.

COFFEE TABLES
A coffee table is a piece of furniture that you seldom notice or pay attention to unless it is missing.

This is because it is the center of many activities in a living room. It is used not only for serving coffee and tea, but also for eating TV meals, storing magazines, doing jigsaw puzzles and playing parlor games. If, therefore, you are tempted to buy a very low coffee table, it is unlikely that it will be as versatile as one that is high enough to eat from or one which you can comfortably lean over while sitting on your sofa to play a board game.

MODERN CIRCULAR
Style Natural wood frame table with marble or glass top.
In use The circular base stands on small rubber feet – it makes a sturdy little table, which is a neat size to fit into the smallest living room.

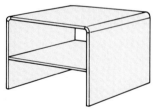

TV SUPPER TABLE
Style Simple solid pine table, high enough to be useful for TV suppers (it stands at approximately sofa-arm height).
In use It has a handy shelf that could be used for storing magazines.

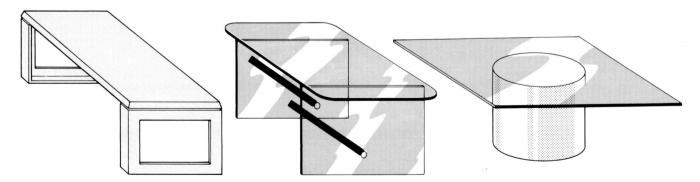

LONG JOHN
Style The long, low, rectangular-shaped table known as the Long John, is still the most popular type of coffee table. It is available in a wide range of materials – one of which is stained ash (above left), another is glass (above right).

In use Stained wood is practical as it camouflages sticky fingermarks and ring marks from coffee cups etc. Glass, on the other hand, is often more bother than it is worth because every little fingermark, stain or speck of dust shows up.

PEDESTAL
Style Smoked glass top resting on drum pedestal base.
In use If you have children, it is advisable to avoid this type as it tends to be unstable.

NESTS OF TABLES

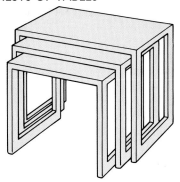 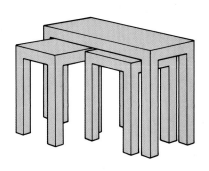 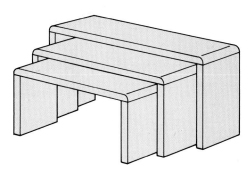

SIMPLE STYLING
Style Very simple shapes fit neatly inside one another.
In use Tables in three 'usable' sizes are a versatile accessory to any room.

MODERN AND BRIGHT
Style Available in bright, high-gloss colors.
In use Two small tables, suitable as lamp tables, nest under a larger table.

SCANDINAVIAN LOOK
Style Solid-wood tables make a feature of the finely crafted jointing.
In use Wide and contoured style is practical and pleasing to the eye.

MAGAZINE/STORAGE TABLES

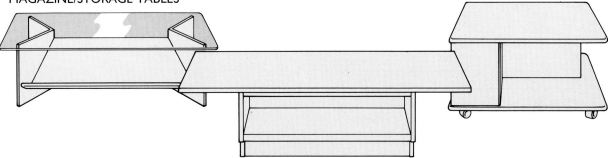

ANGULAR DISPLAY
Style Glass top with beveled edge and rounded corners; angled display shelf.
In use Shelf is edged with beading/lip to house magazines securely.

OPEN STORAGE
Style Tabletop rests on a simple, low drawer shape that is open on one side.
In use Plenty of room for storage of books, magazines and knick knacks.

MOBILE STORAGE
Style Low storage and display units can easily double up as occasional tables.
In use This unit is on casters. It makes an ideal sewing table.

SOFA/LAMP TABLES

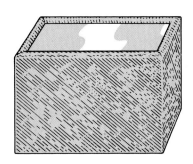 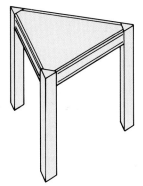 

MODULAR SEATING TABLE UNIT
Style Upholstered table with glass top is part of a run of modular seating.
In use Dust and dirt can collect in the groove between upholstery and glass.

TRIANGULAR SHAPE
Style Triangular, lacquered table.
In use This versatile table is ideal between two seats or at the end of a sofa. Two together make a square table.

RATTAN
Style Rattan side table with glass top over decorative woven rattan.
In use Solid and rigid enough to hold the largest of table lamps.

CONSOLE/SIDE TABLES

▷ **Style** Simple yet interesting console table made in stained ash; the design has a Japanese air to it.
In use Stands tall (30in.) and elegant against any wall – primarily decorative/display purpose.

▷ ▷ **Style** Chipboard table available in various heights and diameters.
In use Designed and made to be draped with floor-length tablecloth and overlay cloth.

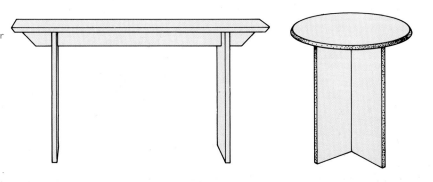

LIVING ROOM STORAGE

The living room needs generous storage to keep clutter at bay and maintain a stylish and streamlined appearance.

Storage furniture is a major investment in any home and, in the living room in particular, it must be organized to cope with the diverse nature of its contents. Finding a place for everything you need within reach is an enormous help in keeping the room looking smart and comfortable for both entertaining and everyday family life.

Every family's storage needs are different so the kind of storage furniture you ultimately choose depends on your budget, lifestyle and type of home. Refer to the checklist above to make sure that you don't forget any essentials at the planning stage.

A well-chosen storage system can enhance the atmosphere of your living room. So while it's important to keep clutter behind closed doors, an element of display to allow you to show off treasured possessions is also essential.

STORAGE CHECKLIST
- ☐ TV and video
- ☐ Stereo system
- ☐ Records, cassettes, CDs, videos
- ☐ Books
- ☐ Newspapers and magazines
- ☐ Stationery, bills, letters
- ☐ Games, playing cards
- ☐ Telephone directories
- ☐ Drinks, glasses
- ☐ China, cutlery
- ☐ Sewing and knitting
- ☐ Ornaments, photographs etc.
- ☐ Plants

Practical and decorative
Living room storage usually includes both open and closed areas. Modular units such as these allow the trivialities of everyday life to be kept safely hidden away, leaving only a charming collection of china and pottery – and the television – on display.

FREESTANDING STORAGE

Freestanding storage units have the obvious advantage of being easy to rearrange and, if you plan to move in the future, you can simply take them with you when you go.

Self-assembly systems are often cheaper than their ready-made counterparts; if you intend to install a storage system to cover an entire wall, a ready-to-assemble unit is much easier to get through the front door! Conversely, this furniture can usually also be dismantled with relative ease if necessary.

Modular systems are well suited to a modest budget and the limited size of many modern living rooms. As well as offering a combination of open and closed modules, they allow you to start off in a small way and add to them as your funds allow or your needs grow. This way, you can tailor your storage to the possessions you already have and the ones you are likely to accumulate.

Single items As well as streamlined storage systems, some rooms look best with a classic combination of freestanding furniture: a roll-top or knee-hole desk for personal items; a sideboard for drinks, dishes and glassware; and a bookcase or glass-fronted cabinet to house books and treasured objects.

Small pieces of specialized furniture – such as coffee tables that include a liquor cabinet underneath, TV and video cabinets, and stereo units with space for an amplifier, cassette deck, records or tapes – can be extremely useful.

▷ *Ample storage*
It is possible to provide plenty of storage without spoiling the atmosphere of a room in which you entertain guests.

Here, storage that almost completely covers an entire wall is broken up by a wall mirror and low table.

A CUMULATIVE APPROACH

Storage furniture need not be purchased all at once – modular systems can 'grow' as needed. Remember to check with the manufacturer that the range will remain on the market.

▽ *Starting off*
At first, only a few units are purchased. Sensibly these have been chosen to include both closed cabinets and open shelves. Arranged along the wall of the room, they provide a sturdy shelf to hold the television.

▽ ▷ *Adding on*
As, perhaps, the family's budget and storage needs grow, extra units can be added. Here, a table top and chair provide a useful work place while taller glass-fronted cupboards allow precious items to remain safe while on show.

▽ ▷ ▷ *The final stage*
Here, the storage system has grown to almost ceiling height. Several of the units have been rearranged to produce a symmetrical arrangement that flanks a large mirror and coffee table.

BRIGHT IDEA

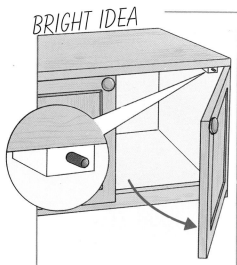

A cabinet light It can be difficult to see into a cabinet, especially one at floor level. A door-operated switch will turn on a light inside the cabinet when the door is opened and can easily be screwed in place under the top of the cabinet; position it so that the closed door depresses the button sufficiently to switch off the light.

BUILT-IN SOLUTIONS

Built-in storage can be as simple as shelving fixed to the walls, or as complex as custom-built units. Either way, building-in represents a long-term investment as the furniture becomes a permanent part of the room.

A 'working wall' of built-in storage can be made to your own specifications, allowing you to choose the shape (perhaps to fill an awkward gap or disguise an eyesore). You can also decide what combination of shelves, closed or glass-fronted cabinet space and special features you want. Built-in units can be traditional, with molded or paneled doors to complement the architectural detail of a period home, or ultra-modern to set the style in a modern room.

Open shelving A living room without shelves can appear rather bare. Family heirlooms, books, photographs and clocks, flowers and plants all need a home where they can be seen and enjoyed, and their color and character make an important contribution to the atmosphere of a room. Open shelving is also extremely versatile because the contents can be altered as the family's

needs change, and easily rearranged to create a fresh new look.

Pre-cut shelves and brackets suitable for DIY installation are available in many different materials, finishes and sizes. Group a number of shelves together for the best effect and keep an eye on proportions – top shelves need to be accessible; narrow shelves are more efficient for display; deeper, well-supported ones are necessary for books, a television, sound system or liquor cabinet. Records need special racks or the support of full-width uprights to prevent them from falling over when just one is removed.

Glass shelving, enhanced by subtle lighting from above, is ideal for showing off delicate collections of china and glass. Resist the temptation to overcrowd as your collections grow.

▽ *Custom-built*
Custom-made storage is a sound investment if you plan to remain in the same home for some time.

This unit made of handsome cherry wood, includes a pass-through to the kitchen, a custom wine rack, a wet bar and a place to fit the microwave oven.

△ A working wall

In an open-plan, a wall storage system can help to create a useful room divider. A plain white finish allows the shelving to merge with the wall behind allowing the decorative knickknacks and small rug to stand out.

It's a good idea to place cabinets rather than open shelving at floor level. Although their contents may be slightly more accessible, low-level open shelving tends to gather dirt and is difficult to keep neat.

▷ Specialized storage

Not everyone possesses a large enough library to merit an entire wall of bookshelves. This alternative arrangement has been designed to incorporate a liquor cabinet with a pull-down door that can double as a serving surface. In addition, this system has been designed to include frequent full-width uprights to prevent all the records falling over if only one is removed. Similarly, shallow shelves provide a home for a cassette collection.

△ Media center

An elaborate modern media center blends into a traditional living room. Arched alcoves installed on either side of the fireplace store and display all video and stereo equipment in shiny gold frames. A movie screen drops down from its hideaway in a ceiling cornice. For a more traditional form of entertainment, reach for a book on one of the shelves underneath.

This room glows with yellow walls and a wood mantel that matches the room's molding. A gold-framed painting above the fireplace tops off this warm decor.

▷ Stylish storage

Although it looks like a single piece of furniture, this stylish oak-veneered storage system is actually made up of modular units that can be put together in many different combinations. Here, a tall glass-fronted central unit flanked by shorter shelves and cabinets makes the storage itself, as well as the items displayed on it, the center of attention.

LIVING ROOM MODULAR STORAGE

Start with just one piece of modular storage furniture and add to it when money and time allow.

A modular storage system consists of a series of basic matching shapes of compatible size and style. It gives you plenty of freedom to buy as much or as little as you require. Choose from cabinets, shelves, TV/stereo storage units and so on. The flexibility of these systems means they have become more popular with the household than single free-standing pieces (covered in the following chapter).

FEATURES CHECKLIST
Before buying modular storage, check which features you require:
- ☐ Illuminated shelves suitable for displaying glass and china.
- ☐ Flap-down cabinets suitable as cocktail or liquor cabinets.
- ☐ Glass doors – smoked or clear.
- ☐ Units for TV/stereo equipment, record, CD and tape storage.
- ☐ Corner units so furniture can run along more than one wall.
- ☐ Space-saving units that house stowaway beds or tables/desks.

WOOD-VENEERED FURNITURE
Furniture made of solid wood is very expensive and therefore quite rare these days. A much cheaper alternative to solid wood is veneered wood.

With this method the manufacturer makes the body/carcase of a piece of furniture from either plywood, medium density fiberboard or chipboard and then covers the outer surface with a layer of veneer. Veneer is a layer of wood thin cut to make the most of a wood's decorative grain. Real wood veneers are expensive and are often replaced by various man-made laminates and what are known as foils, which are either paper or PVC sheets printed with a wood-effect pattern.

FINISHES
The finish on wooden furniture, whether solid wood or veneered, can make a big difference to its appearance. It may be stained a darker-than-natural shade or tinted to look old. Some wood can also be treated to look lighter or lacquered for a tough, glossy finish.

TYPES OF WOOD
Below is a list of the most popular woods used for furniture – modular storage units included.

Ash A pale, straight-grained wood; stained black.

Beech Pale to mid-brown, fine grain.

Burr-woods The woods of ornately veneered furniture may be referred to as burr-elm, burr-walnut, etc. This means the wood is taken from irregular growth, usually at the tree base, used for its highly figured markings.

Cherry Close-grained, pale-colored, hard fruitwood.

Curl-woods A wood with the prefix curl before it, such as curl-mahogany, refers to wood taken from the joint of trunk and branch, or two branches.

Elm Yellow-brown; large, open grain.

Mahogany Deep reddish brown, straight grain with subtle striping. (Sapele is similar with regular stripes.)

Maple Tones of medium to reddish brown; often children's furniture.

Oak Lightish natural tone with deep open grain – very strong.

Pine Red pine from Russia is regarded by furniture makers as the best pine – light pinkish-red color, close grain. Much furniture described as pine today is, in fact, often made from one of the many inferior, cheaper softwoods.

Rosewood Rare dark wood with deep pinkish-violet undertones.

Teak Mid-golden brown, smooth with mostly straight grain (Iroko is similar, but coarser).

Walnut American walnut is a coffee brown color and has purple patches. English walnut has black patches, and is high quality, scarce and expensive.

TYPES OF UNITS

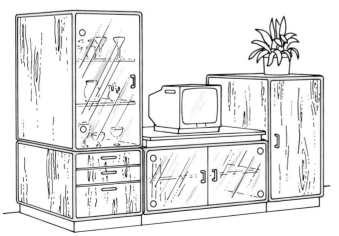

MODERN FREESTANDING
Style This is a storage system offering a wide choice of units that differ in style and height.

In use Putting tall cabinets alongside lower base units creates an interesting arrangement and gives you a natural position for the TV and stereo equipment. Optional glass doors and/or glass shelves transform an ordinary storage unit into an ideal display cabinet for glass and china.

TRADITIONAL-STYLE FREESTANDING
Style The modern concept of modular storage units is reproduced in an elegant period-style look. Ornate handles, paneled doors and leaded glass cabinets all add to the traditional look.

In use A system of units that are all the same height offer a neat ceiling-to-floor run of storage.
There are corner units too, so the run can extend to more than just one wall

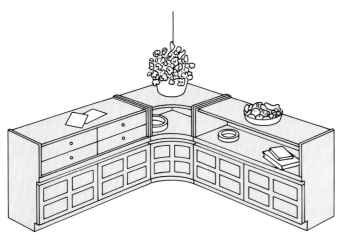

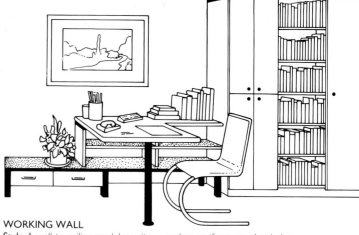

BASE UNITS

Style An alternative to the traditional sideboard.

In use Low floor-standing units of varying widths and identical heights provide open or enclosed storage space and surfaces for ornaments or TV and stereo equipment. Corner units come with convex- or concave-shaped fascias. A run of base units is ideal if you prefer uncluttered walls or need picture-hanging space.

WORKING WALL

Style A wall-to-ceiling modular unit that offers you more than just storage space.

In use Units around the desk provide storage for books, files, pens and pencils, but can quite easily be used to store table linen and so on if you use the desk as a dining table.

Watchpoint Remember that units supported on legs are likely to make dents in carpets and other floorcoverings.

WALL-HANGING UNITS

Style Ideal for smaller rooms as they do not take up floor space. Arrange them in straight rows or at different heights.

In use Both bottom and top units are fixed by cantilevered brackets, which go deep into the wall for adequate support.

Watchpoint Avoid hanging units at the bottom, this makes it tricky to vacuum the carpet.

BED-SIT UNIT

Style A modular unit ideal for a studio apartment or a living room that doubles as a bedroom.

In use A cabinet fascia folds down to reveal a hide-away bed, which can simply be let down to lie at right-angles to the unit, or, if space is limited, can turn through 90° so it lies alongside units. Closets can be used as wardrobes or can be fitted with shelves.

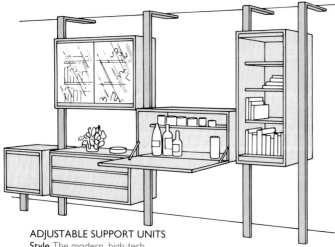

ADJUSTABLE SUPPORT UNITS

Style The modern, high-tech modular equivalent of adjustable shelving units.

In use Metal supports (which come in a variety of lengths) stand on the floor and are fixed at the top to the wall or ceiling. Storage units then slide up and down these supports, so you can put them at desired positions. These can be used against the wall or as a room divider.

CHECKLIST BEFORE BUYING

☐ Plan carefully before buying any storage units, listing what you need to store in appropriate groups.

☐ Use a grid and measurements drawn to scale to plan out the combinations, remembering you can add on later.

☐ Do not forget to take into account where the wires are going to run from TV, lamps and so on.

☐ Consider how difficult some features might be to clean – cleaning leaded lattice work glass fronts, dusting intricate carving or open shelves is sometimes awkward.

☐ Consider whether the style might date easily.

☐ Examine a sample of what you are going to buy. Pay particular attention to the insides of drawers and backs of cabinets. Open and close items and make sure that they are stable.

☐ Check what care the units require, such as – waxing, polishing or just wiping over with a damp cloth, to maintain the finish.

☐ Check the length of the guarantee.

CHOOSING BOOKCASES AND DISPLAY CABINETS

It pays to choose the right furniture to house books and cherished ornaments.

CHECKLIST

Before buying bookcases or display cabinets, consider the features you may require:

☐ Wall-hung or floor standing
☐ Optimum height
☐ Open or closed shelves
☐ Sliding or conventional-opening doors
☐ Glazed or solid door
☐ Depth of shelves
☐ Adjustable shelves
☐ Drawers
☐ Dual-purpose: doubling up as coffee table, telephone shelf
☐ Integral lighting
☐ Glass shelves/sides
☐ Mirrored backing for the shelves
☐ Lockable doors to secure valuables and to keep out prying small fingers

One advantage that single bookcases and display cabinets have over modular storage furniture, as described on pages 67-68, is that they are more likely to fit into other rooms in your home should your requirements change or should you decide to move. Basically, single pieces are easier to move around because they are less complicated and not tailor-made for a specific length of wall or a certain ceiling height. Also, they can usually be moved without having to be dismantled.

Minus points However, the disadvantage of single pieces compared to modular storage furniture is that for the amount of space taken up in a room there is less actual storage/shelf/display area. You can offset this by choosing pieces of furniture that have a definite decorative value in their own right and therefore deserve the space that they take up.

Buying old You may be able to find suitable items secondhand, through classified advertisements in newspapers, in junk shops or at furniture auctions. Older items may require renovation, but can be relatively cheap to buy and should be worth any time and money spent on restoration.

Old furniture tends to have a character that is difficult to find in new items, and especially suits older houses or period-style decoration.

Safety Whether you buy new or secondhand, always remember that bookcases and display cabinets must be stable. This is particularly important if you have small children who could be injured by collapsing pieces of furniture full of heavy books or china and fragile glassware.

Materials and styles Bookcases and display cabinets are mostly made from wood – either solid wood or plywood, chipboard or fiberboard covered with a thin layer of wood veneer. Alternatively some modern designs are covered with man-made laminated finishes. They come in a variety of shapes and sizes from traditional to more off-beat designs. Whatever you buy, it should fit in with your room decor.

STYLES OF BOOKCASES

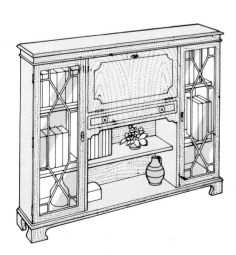

BOOK/LIQUOR CABINET

Style Shelves at each end of this wooden bookcase are fully adjustable and enclosed by Gothic-style beaded glass doors. The inner section contains a liquor cabinet that has a mirrored back and a fall-front door. Below this there is a drawer and two open shelves.
In use Versatile and functional, the cabinet is 58in. wide×12½in. deep×74in. high.

LIBRARY-STYLE

Style A wooden bookcase comprises a base unit of cabinet and drawers and a top unit of adjustable shelves with glazed doors.
In use This style can create a traditional 'library' look in any living room or study. It stands 77in. high, 40in. wide and 15in. deep. For the relatively small amount of floor space it takes up, it provides a lot of storage room.

MODERN SLIDING

Style Compact, wood-veneered bookcase that incorporates shelves and drawers behind sliding glass doors. The middle shelf is adjustable, so most sizes of book can be accommodated.
In use Slimline enough (12in. deep, 40in. wide, 42in. high) to be unobtrusive in any room.
Watchpoint Each time the doors are opened or even touched, fingerprints will mark the glass.

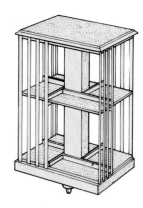

WATERFALL

Style This is called a waterfall book/display shelf because of its attractive appearance – it's narrower at the top than at the bottom.
In use Open wooden shelves suitable for housing books, ornaments or other knickknacks. It stands 46in. high making it the right height to double up as a bedside cabinet.

BOOK TROUGH

Style Simple open wooden shelving. Shelves are angled so that book spines face upwards slightly. This means you can see, at a glance, all the book titles and their authors – handy for older or disabled people.
In use This book trough measures 32in. wide×12in. deep×30in. high.

REVOLVER

Style Revolving wooden bookcase.
In use Such a bookcase should not be placed flush against a wall as it needs room to revolve. This makes books easily accessible from both sides (front and back) of the bookcase. It stands 33in. high, 20in. wide and 20in. deep.

STYLES OF DISPLAY CABINETS

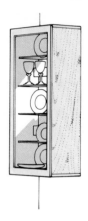

MODERN DISPLAY SHELVES

Style This modern open shelving unit in fashionable stained or lacquered wood is suitable for displaying ornaments, china or books.
In use As well as storage shelves, it can also serve as a low room divider. It measures 72in. wide×12in. deep×31in. high, but is available in a larger size. Its shape makes it easy to clean.

REPRODUCTION QUEEN ANNE

Style Reproduction wood-veneered display case with Queen Anne-style cabriole legs. The doors are glass, as are the sides of the cabinet and the shelves (which are mirror-backed).
In use An abundance of glass shows off prized pieces. It is 36in. wide, 18in. deep and 60in. high. Drawer is ideal for cutlery.

WALL-HUNG

Style Wall-hung wooden display cabinet with glass shelves, glazed doors and internal lighting.
In use It keeps good china and other breakables well out of children's reach. It measures about 24in. wide×14in. deep×48in. high.
Watchpoint Make sure it is well secured, preferably on cantilevered brackets.

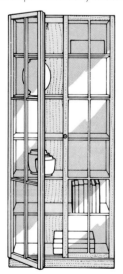
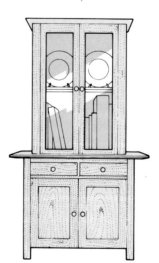

HIGH RISE

Style Modern, tall, glass-fronted cabinet with three fixed and two adjustable shelves. It is wood-veneered, available lacquered or stained.
In use As this piece is so tall (35in. wide×17½in. deep×77in. high), it stands on a flat plinth rather than on legs, which gives it extra stability and wastes no space.

TWO-PIECE

Style Wood-veneered cabinet made up of a separate top and base unit like the traditional dresser. Top shelving unit is 36in. wide×16in. deep×44in. high. Base shelving unit is 45½in. ×18in.×33½in. Both available open or enclosed.
In use An attractive piece that doesn't display contents – but can hide a multitude of objects.

HIGH-TECH

Style This tubular metal shelving unit is supplied in a black, white or metallic gray painted finish for the latest high-tech look.
In use It stands 73½in. high, 26½in. wide and 15in. deep. The shelves are made from perforated sheets of metal. Look for trolleys and chairs that match this style. Easy to clean.

AUDIO-VISUAL STORAGE UNITS

There is a wide choice of storage units available, specifically made to house TVs, VCRs and stereo gear.

Many living room modular storage ranges offer a module for TV set, video recorder and stereo equipment, but there is also a huge number of stand-alone furniture pieces that are specifically designed to house these items.

High-tech, modern homes make a virtue out of their viewing and listening equipment and choose it to suit the style and decoration of the room.

However, in period settings and traditionally furnished homes, the overwhelming modern style of audio-visual systems tends to spoil the atmosphere. Consequently, some people try to hide the equipment completely, while others prefer a compromise of convenience and looks.

Buying to fit TV sets are much smaller than they used to be, but it is impossible to generalize on size. Many people have a large set downstairs and a smaller one (often portable) for kitchen and bedroom viewing. The only way to tell if a unit is the right size for your TV is by measuring it.

As for the size of stereo equipment, there is even more variation; mini- and midi-stack systems, ones made up of independent components (amplifier, CD, tape deck and turntable) and music centers (one component and speakers).

If possible, choose an audio-visual housing system that is adaptable; this could be a unit with adjustable shelves or one big and versatile enough to accommodate combinations of equipment in the event of a change of equipment.

Style When it comes to a unit's appearance, there is plenty of choice. Reproduction, period and contemporary styles in wood finishes – natural and stained, and high-tech fashion units.

UNITS FOR TV AND VIDEO RECORDERS

The most important thing about a TV and video storage unit is that it should be placed where the screen can be seen easily. Experts say the ideal viewing height is a minimum 18in.

Size When buying a unit, check it is the right size and height to house your TV and ensure it is suitable for your video recorder. Front-loading video recorders don't need to be moved for normal operation, but top-loading models need a slide-out shelf below the TV or a space above so there is access for loading video cassettes.

Ventilation Most TV cabinets have ventilation slots in the back of them, others are even backless – if a unit is completely enclosed make sure it is at least 6in. deeper than the TV.

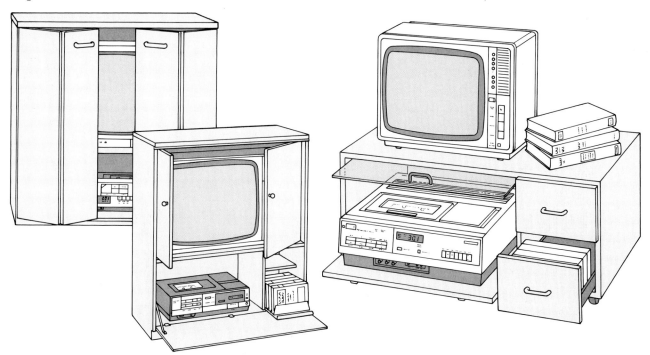

ENCLOSED TV AND VIDEO CABINETS

Style The TV is usually fitted into the unit and can be covered by a pair of doors, when not in use. And there is usually storage space (a shelf or slide-out tray) below for a video recorder. Occasionally, there is room for it above. Choose between the more classical piece of furniture that looks to all intents

and purposes like a liquor cabinet (above right), and the more modern wooden hide-away cabinet (above left) with concertina-style folding doors.

In use The doors may have special hinges to allow them to open flush with the sides of the cabinet or slide inside the cabinet itself.

OPEN TV, ENCLOSED VIDEO STORAGE

Style The TV sits on top of the unit while the video recorder is stored below, behind an up-and-over door or straightforward opening doors. The internal shelf may have a slide-out action (to give access to a top-loading video recorder). The area should allow for tape storage or there should be a separate drawer

or compartment for tapes.

In use A glass or transparent up-and-over door keeps dust off the video recorder, but still allows you to see the digital read-out on the recorder telling you what it is recording, how it is programed and it also enables you to see the digital time clock.

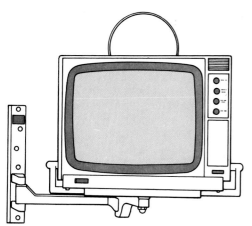

◁ **TV WALL BRACKET**
Style Steel support bracket swivels so you can position TV as desired. It has an adjustable base plate for it to hold different sized TV sets.
In use This can be screwed to the wall or ceiling and keeps the TV out of the way of children and pets.

▷ **OPEN TROLLEY STORAGE**
Style A modern three-tiered tubular metal trolley with perforated metal shelves.
In use An ideal (and relatively cheap) way to house a portable or small TV set and video recorder.

STEREO EQUIPMENT

Choosing storage units for audio equipment requires more care than for TV and video recorders, because there are more parts to consider. Measure each piece of equipment that has to go in the unit and then work out where they are to be positioned. It is disastrous if you buy a unit and then have to cram everything into it when you get it home.

Everyday access Consider how you use the equipment and if there is adequate access to it – most stereo systems require access from the front and top. (Bear in mind that most turntable decks have opening lids, but tape decks and compact discs can be loaded from the front or top.) Operating height is important. They should be low so you can kneel or high so you can stand while loading tapes and so on. Avoid sizes in between. A few storage units include room for speakers. These look neat, but aren't necessarily the best position for speakers, so consult an audio dealer before buying if you are concerned about optimum sound quality.

Wiring Most stereo units have pre-drilled holes in their backs for wires. Electrical equipment should always have adequate ventilation – leave enclosed units open during operation.

△ **ENCLOSED CABINET**
Style Usually with lifting lid and door-front opening, which may be disguised as a mock drawer-front. A fall-flap front is another alternative.
In use The ultimate disguise, and some say good for fooling prospective burglars. Keep open when in use.
Watchpoint It limits choice if you plan to change equipment.

STACKING STORAGE
Style Space-saving, modern high-rise unit specifically designed for a stacking stereo system.
In use Most stacking types are fully enclosed with opening and lifting tinted glass doors. Shelves are adjustable to hold most stereo systems. Casters allow easy positioning of the unit in your home.

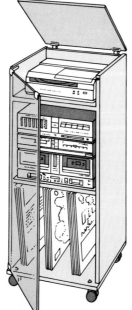

ALL-ROUNDERS
Style This is a modular storage system made up of single units specifically for audio-visual equipment. It has various degrees of enclosure and disguise for stereo, TV, videos and speakers.
In use Very versatile, you can add more units to it as you acquire extra equipment, records and so on.

STORAGE FOR ACCESSORIES

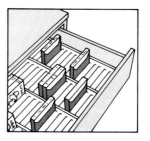

It is very handy when buying an audio-visual storage unit to have additional storage for LPs, tapes, video cassettes and compact discs. Look for drawers that are lined with slotted trays to hold tapes and discs (see above left). This enables you to keep them in order.

Record racks are standard with most stereo storage units. The unit shown (above right) is a single piece of furniture solely for records. The neat, slide-in, slide-out cabinet (rather like the sort found in a built-in kitchen) allows you to find a record at the back without having to take out those in front first.

MEDIA ROOMS: SOUND AND VISION

TV, video, stereo, and compact disc: how to get the best from your home entertainment system.

Speakers should be positioned so that they give the best possible sound. Where you place the speakers – and, therefore, the quality of sound produced, depends, to a large extent, on the shape of the room and the type of speaker cabinet – some are designed to sit on the floor, others on a bookshelf.

Soft furnishings also affect sound quality. **Positioning speakers** The loudness of the sound (particularly the bass sounds) coming out of a speaker is influenced by where it is placed. The loudest position is on the floor (or on the ceiling) in the corner of a room. Here, the sound output is being helped by the two walls of

the corner and the surface of the floor (or ceiling). The next loudest position is on the floor (or ceiling) against one wall; here the sound is being helped by only one wall and the surface of the floor (or ceiling). The further away the speaker is from the ideal corner, the quieter it becomes.

In a small room, the speakers are often so close to the seating that it is impossible to have background music without it interfering with conversation. In such a case, mounting the speakers off the floor – on a shelf, or on one of a variety of floor or wall stands available – can help.

Some very expensive speakers are supplied with detailed instructions as to where they should be placed for optimum listening. It's a good idea to follow these instructions faithfully as they are usually the result of exhaustive listening tests by the designers.

Soft furnishings, such as carpets, curtains and a lot of upholstered furniture, can affect the quality of sound from the speakers dramatically.

A 'live' room has bare walls and floors that reflect the sound, making it much brighter, bigger and louder compared with a 'dead' room – one with fitted carpets and curtains. In an extreme case, a 'live' room can echo and confuse the sound, whereas a 'dead' room can make the sound seem small, dull and soft.

▷ *Serious listening*
If a line is drawn from the center of the cone of sound coming from each speaker, the point where the two lines cross is the optimum position. For really serious listening, the distance between the two speakers must equal the distance between each speaker and the listener, forming a triangle of equal sides.

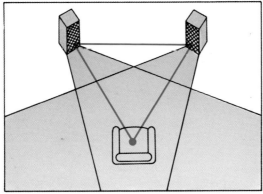

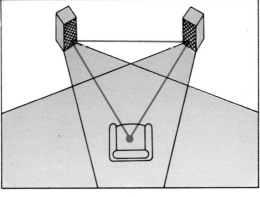

△ *Whole room sound*
Speakers facing diagonally into a squarish room from the corners of one wall give whole-room sound.

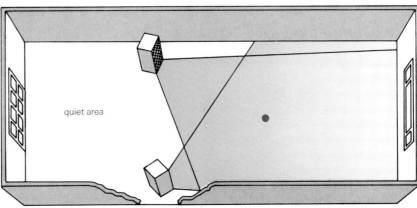

quiet area

△ *Rectangular room with quiet area*
A long room can be more difficult to position speakers in successfully, but it is also more versatile. If you want a

quiet area in the room, for dining or study, for example, place one or both speakers partway down the wall, facing into the listening area.

POSITIONING THE TV

A television must be easy to view from the most comfortable seats, but it shouldn't dominate the room. This seemingly conflicting set of conditions can be met by having the TV on a trolley, or keeping it in a cabinet or cupboard with closing doors.

Make sure the TV is positioned so that reflection off the screen from windows and lighting is avoided as much as possible. The recommended minimum height from the base of the set to the floor is about 18in. This ensures that good seating posture is maintained. Unfortunately, most commercial stands are much lower than this, forcing the viewers to crane their necks down and forward or slump in the seat in order to see the screen.

It is a good idea to have some lighting near the TV when viewing. This is because looking away from the screen from time to time helps to reduce the eye fatigue caused by focusing on the small screen for a long time. This relief is most effective if you look at something of a similar brightness to the screen – otherwise your eyes have to readjust whenever the lighting conditions change.

CENTRAL CONTROL

The main stereo unit is the amplifier, if it is combined with a radio tuner it is known as a receiver. The amplifier receives low-level signals from the turntable, radio tuner, cassette deck, CD player, video and so on, and boosts them to a sufficient level to drive the speakers.

Connecting your system Most of the connections made are between and among the amplifier and the above units, so it is a good idea to keep them all together to avoid trailing wires.

If your video recorder is stereo, it is worth connecting it to the amplifier along with all the main units. This allows you to listen to video cassettes in stereo; you can also channel TV programs through the speakers.

Most amplifiers have three or four outlets marked:
- phono, which is for the turntable only;
- tape for the cassette deck;
- tuner and/or aux, which can be used for radio, CD, video or any additional unit you want to connect.

Power and connections If you do not have enough electrical outlets near the amplifier and other equipment, it's a good idea to plug everything into a fused adaptor strip socket. Sometimes the amplifier has built-in outlets providing power for additional units such as the turntable or CD player. This enables them all to be turned on and off with one switch and cuts down on the number of the wall outlets you will need.

Once your equipment is arranged in position and set up, the only remaining connections to be made are:
- the speaker cables;
- the cable from the video to the TV;
- and the cable(s) from the FM/TV antenna or indoor antennas to the tuner and video unit.

If you need longer speaker cables than those provided by the manufacturer, use a thick stranded or automotive cable, as this will preserve sound quality over the longer distance. Long cables suitable for the video unit/TV and tuner to antenna socket interconnections are readily obtainable from most video and stereo shops.

Block diagram of suitable wiring scheme

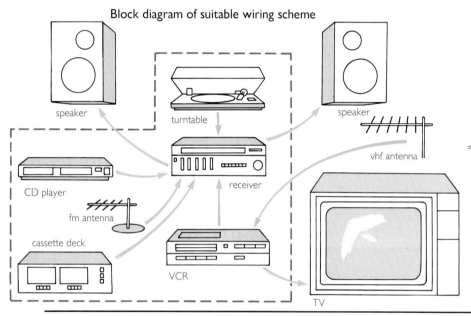

speaker, turntable, speaker, vhf antenna, CD player, receiver, fm antenna, cassette deck, VCR, TV

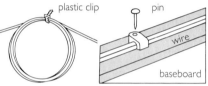

◁ *Connecting your system*
Most connections are made between the units inside the dotted line. If they are kept together, the wires and plugs can be neatly ordered and concealed. The speakers and TV can be positioned anywhere you like in the room.

plastic clip   pin
wire
baseboard

△ *Keeping wires neat*
Run cables close to baseboards and pin them with plastic clips. Never twist or bend wires; wind unnecessary lengths in a loose circle and secure with a plastic grip.

CARE AND STORAGE

Always leave enough room around and above the turntable to allow the lid to be opened and records changed. Similarly, allow space above any other top-loading units, such as some videos, cassette decks, and CD players so that they may be loaded and unloaded.

To prevent units from overheating, it is important to leave enough space above and below them for air to circulate; for this reason, don't leave record covers or magazines on top of any electrical equipment that is switched on. If video or stereo units are mounted in a cabinet, make sure the doors are open when the units are operating.

The main enemy of records, cassettes, and compact discs is heat from the sun, a gas or electric fire, or even a video or stereo unit. Records buckle or warp in heat, and it causes magnetic tape, including audio and video cassettes, gradually to become erased. Moisture can also cause damage, so always ensure that your records and tapes are stored in a cool,

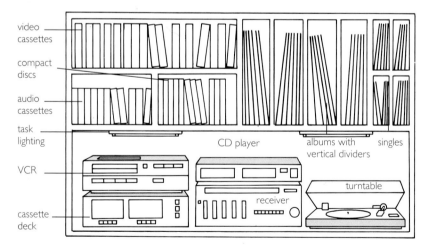

video cassettes, compact discs, audio cassettes, task lighting, VCR, cassette deck, CD player, albums with vertical dividers, singles, receiver, turntable

dry, clean place.

Stack records vertically with the spines facing outwards, and use dividers to break them up into groups of twenty or so. This allows easy access and, more important, means that they have no weight on them as they would in a horizontal pile. Audio and video cassettes and compact discs are also best stacked vertically for ease of access.

There are a number of units designed specially for record and tape storage, or you can simply treat them as you would books and build a series of shelves. Storage at eye-level is a good idea to avoid a frenzied search for a favorite record or tape. Avoid using the same shelf for the turntable and storage, otherwise the stylus will jump every time you touch an album.

LIGHTING YOUR LIVING ROOM

The way you light your living room is as important as how you decorate it, so the subject merits serious thought.

Good lighting is a vital ingredient in any room and particularly a living room. There is more to it than hanging a single lamp in the middle of the room and leaving it at that. But it can be quite difficult to decide what you need and how to achieve a pleasing and practical result.

There's really no point in spending a lot of time and cash on decoration, furniture and furnishings and ignoring the lighting. After all, you probably spend as much, possibly more, of your time seeing the room by artificial lighting than you do by natural light.

You can change the whole look of the room with clever lighting – and it may be a much cheaper option than redecorating. Use it to create atmosphere with light and shade, for specific tasks such as reading, and to make the best of your decoration.

Lighting is about decoration too. Floor and table lamps, wall lights and ceiling pendants all contribute to the style of the room – choose lights for their looks as well as the quality of light they produce.

Versatility A living room is where a variety of different activities take place. So plan the lighting to be as versatile as possible.

Dimmer switches, which allow you to adjust the level of lighting to suit the mood and the activities taking place, are an excellent investment. You can turn the lights right up for all-over illumination, or down for a cozy feel, with perhaps table lamps providing intimate pools of light.

Several table and floor lamps are a flexible way of providing a variety of lighting options – different combinations producing different effects.

Think of your living room as a stage – bathe it in light when you want a bright effect, turn the lighting down to create a mood, use table lamps to light specific areas where activities such as reading, doing homework or watching TV take place.

Flexible arrangement
Decorative matching wall lights and low-hung pendant in this living room can be used together for overall illumination or to give separate pools of light. Dimmers add to the possibilities. For instance, you can lower the wall lights to bring the table into prominence or vice versa. The adjustable floor task lamp can be positioned for reading in any part of the room, while the large table lamp creates another cozy oasis.

CREATING A MOOD

When planning living room lighting, think about how you use the room and choose the lighting with function very much in mind – reading and entertaining, for instance, require very different light levels. Do you entertain here a lot, use it for general family life – or a combination of the two? If you read, work or watch TV in it, where are the lights in relation to the furniture? Are there pictures or objects you want to highlight?

Another consideration is atmosphere. Do you want the living room to be intimate and cozy, bright and efficient, or have different moods for different occasions? Remember to use shadow as well as light to create atmosphere.

Different areas of a room can be lit in different ways and brought into prominence according to the activities at the time. So several sources of adjustable lighting are invaluable. For instance, when you are alone in the room reading, then the area you are in can be lit by a table lamp or possibly a floor lamp, with or without general background lighting. When entertaining, the floor lamp can be moved behind the

◁ *Low light*
This nighttime living room is geared more towards conversation than reading or working.

The candlestick wall lights with low-wattage bulbs (between 15 and 60w) provide a little general light but not enough to destroy the gentle atmosphere. The fire is the center of life around which the furniture is grouped; table lamps cast pools of light, creating interesting shadows and leaving the rest of the richly painted room gently out of focus.

▽ *Highlights*
The same room given a different treatment; one more suited to reading or hobbies such as sewing.

Recessed eyeball fixtures in the ceiling highlight the pictures in the corner by the fireplace while the table lamp at the other end of the sofa provides light for reading.

Two separate lighting circuits – each controlled by a dimmer switch – are wired in to give versatility. One controls the eyeballs directed towards the pictures; the other deals with the table lights and the eyeball that is trained on the chimney breast.

Shelf light A shelf for ornaments becomes more interesting if illuminated. Mount a small strip light behind a furring strip, under the front of the shelf above the one you want to display. Run the wire down one of the back corners and plug into an electrical outlet.

sofa, placing the occupants in soft focus and leaving the rest of the room in shadow.

While lighting levels are very important in creating a mood, a simple but often forgotten way of providing atmospheric light is with candles. An ordinary room can be transformed into something quite mysterious, bathed in the soft, warm light of flickering candles.

LIGHTING POINTS

While flexibility is the key to good living room lighting, your choices will, of course, be determined by cost and by how easy they are to install.

Plug-in fixtures – table and floor lamps, uplighters, and so on – are the easiest from an installation point of view, as long as you have enough electrical outlets.

If you want to install a completely new system, inevitably there will be some rewiring to be done. Wall lights can be installed wherever you like, although you will have to redecorate over the new plasterwork where wires have been snaked in. Floor and table lamp outlets can be wired to a single switch by the door, so that they can all be turned on and off easily.

Fixtures such as downlighters and directional eyeballs are often recessed into the ceiling. You may not be able to do this, however, because of the type of ceiling – there may not be enough space above it, for instance. And some people, quite rightly, are unwilling to cut into a fine period ceiling.

Surface-mounted downlighters or directional spots are alternatives; the latter are, on the whole, much more attractive than they used to be.

Track lighting is another good idea for a living room; it provides a flexible system, enabling you to use a variety of fixtures. Tracks come in a variety of styles and finishes – the best approach is to choose an unobtrusive one, unless you deliberately want to make a feature out of it.

Finally, don't forget dimmers. They're easy to install and are invaluable because you can brighten or darken the room at the turn of a switch.

▷ *Overall illumination*
Downlighters in the ceiling provide good overall light in this living room. The table lamps, which create separate pools of light, are used to create a warm atmosphere. Floor-to-ceiling mirrors on either side of the fireplace double the effect of whatever lights are on.

▽ *Clever disguise*
Here, background lighting is provided by wall uplighters either side of the chimney breast; they bounce light off the ceiling and the mirror above the fireplace. These wall lights are made from plaster and can be painted to blend with the walls. There is also a reading lamp on one side table and a floor lamp that can be moved wherever it is needed.

◁ *Uncluttered attic*
An attic living room with streamlined lighting to complement an airy, uncluttered decorative scheme.

Recessed adjustable eyeballs direct light just where it is needed – onto the painting, to wash the walls, to highlight the coffee table or towards the seating.

▽ *Mixed lighting*
A variety of light fixtures brighten this green-and-yellow color scheme. The ceiling lamp provides general lighting, and a desk lamp produces the proper amount of light for working. Candles are available for a more romantic or relaxed mood.

▷ *Highlights and shadows*
A good example of how a carefully chosen modern floor lamp can perfectly complement period architecture. The tall chrome torchere throws light onto the gloss-painted wall above it, leaving the rest of the room fairly shadowy. The lamp subtly emphasizes the height and features of the room, without distracting attention from the glow of candles and firelight.

▽ *Standard direction*
The generous wide-angled shades on these floor lamps direct light down onto the sofa. The classically modern style of the lamps is very much in keeping with the plain room and streamlined furniture.

◁ *Background for viewing*
A series of glass shelves for books and ornaments is bathed in light from above, giving the display a warm attractive glow.

As well as creating an interesting focal point, this practical solution makes the shelves a subtle light source when the TV is on, and the round ball light turned off.

LAMPS AND SHADES
Floor and table lamps can create atmosphere, provide background light or direct light on activities.

Good lighting is essential so it is important to choose the right equipment.

This chapter covers freestanding light sources (table lamps, desk lights and floor lights). These are plug-in lamps run off an electrical outlet so they are easy to install and portable. This makes them an ideal choice if you require equipment or if you are not prepared to rewire for permanent fixtures.

Freestanding lights are, however, best avoided in young children's rooms where they might easily get knocked over. The next two chapters cover ceiling-mounted and wall-mounted fixtures (including spotlights, fluorescent strips, downlighters and uplighters) so that you will know what is available when you come to planning the lighting scheme for any room.

The style of lighting should be compatible with the style of a room but, most important, you should work out what you want any individual light to do and where it will be positioned in relation to other lights. There are three main types of lighting:

Background lighting provides a general view of visibility. It is indirect, restful and a replacement for natural light.

Task lighting is strong localized lighting that provides illumination for specific activities and includes work lights and guiding lights (e.g. on a stairwell).

Decorative lighting is used to accent or highlight attractive objects in a room and to create atmosphere/effects.

Most rooms require a combination of the first two types, and in general living areas you may also want to add some decorative lighting to spotlight a picture or mementoes.

CHECKLIST
Here is a checklist of points to consider when deciding what kind of lighting you want. Appearance and cost will, of course, also play a part.
☐ What is the style of the room – traditional or modern?
☐ What atmosphere or mood are you aiming to create?
☐ What is the room primarily used for – relaxed conversation and reading, sleeping, studying, craftwork, household tasks?
☐ Do activities move around and require flexible lighting?
☐ Is there space for freestanding lights?
☐ Do you want to highlight plants, paintings or mementoes?

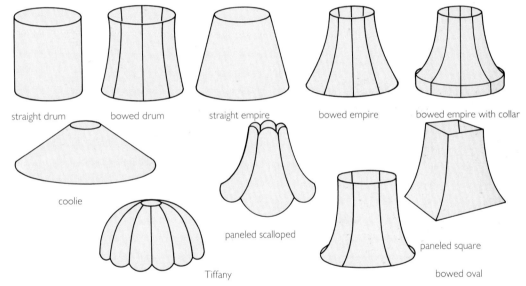

straight drum   bowed drum   straight empire   bowed empire   bowed empire with collar

coolie

paneled scalloped

paneled square

Tiffany

bowed oval

TABLE LAMPS
A table lamp provides a warm, intimate glow and is primarily used for low-level background lighting. It is a useful supplement to other lights in living rooms, bedrooms and hallways and is often a decorative object in itself.

Depending on the amount of light thrown downwards by the shade, a table lamp can also be used for task lighting (for armchair reading or as a conventional bedside lamp) or for display lighting (to illuminate a table display of favorite objects for example).

Shades with open tops can also bounce light off the ceiling.

The bases and shades can be bought separately or together.

TRADITIONAL TABLE LAMPS
Style Bases and shades come in a variety of styles suitable for both traditional and modern furnished rooms. Simple pottery bases look good in both settings and so do candlestick, greek urn and some Chinese styles.

As a general rule, the simpler the shade the more suitable it will be for a modern decor.

In use Choose a fine 2-ply electric wire rather than a bulky 3-ply wire when wiring up a lamp.

Watchpoint A shade contributes to the color of the light produced when lit so it is best to see it illuminated before buying. The shade must be in the right proportion to the base and deep enough to shield the light bulb.

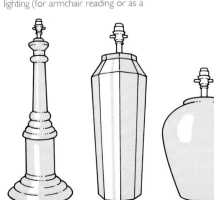

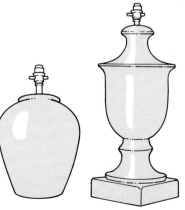

candlestick   column   ginger jar   urn   Chinese vase   spice jar   small globe

DECORATIVE TABLE LIGHTS

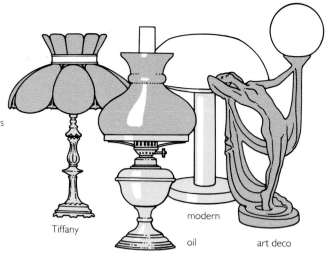

ART NOUVEAU TIFFANY LAMP
Style A colored, stained glass shade on an ornate metal base. There are several variations on the basic petal shade. This old-style opulence adds a decorative touch best suited to traditional settings.

ART DECO TABLE LAMP
Style This design must be used with care, but can look equally at home in a modern home as well as a 30s-style room. The base often consists of a draped female figure holding a globe-shaped shade.

In use The lamp provides general lighting and, at the same time, is a very distinctive object.

OIL LAMP
Style A brass lamp with a frosted, etched or clear glass shade, which is best suited to cottage and country settings.
In use New oil lamps are available converted to electricity – old ones can easily be adapted.

MODERN TABLE LAMP
Style A range of styles usually with a streamlined look.

Tiffany

modern

oil

art deco

FLOOR LAMPS

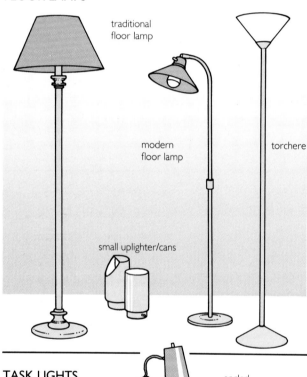

traditional floor lamp

modern floor lamp

torchere

small uplighter/cans

These give general background lighting, and some can also be used for task lighting.

Use mainly in living rooms and dining rooms (and possibly hallways) and position near a wall or next to furniture and away from traffic areas.

CONVENTIONAL FLOOR
Style This traditional light looks pretty in rooms or more formal in a traditional setting, depending on the type of shade. Use larger versions of those on previous page.
In use Provides a pool of light for reading when set beside or some way behind a chair.
Watchpoint Look for a sturdy base and keep wire well away from circulation routes.

MODERN FLOOR
Style Simple, stark lines suit most furnishing styles and particularly those with a contemporary look.
In use More versatile than the

floor lamp, they can often be angled, raised or lowered.
Watchpoint Ask to see the lamp lit before buying so that you can check whether glare is a problem when you are seated.

TORCHERE
Style The streamlined, vertical lines of torcheres are mainly suitable for modern settings.
In use Most of the beam is bounced off the ceiling to achieve a soft background glow. Best reflected off white or pale-colored surfaces.
Watchpoint Should be tall enough to shield bulb and avoid glare at sitting and standing level. Needs a stable base.

SMALL UPLIGHTER/CAN
Style Unobtrusive modern shape is suitable for any setting.
In use Position behind a sofa, low table or plants to flood the walls with light.
Watchpoint Do not place too close to plants.

TASK LIGHTS

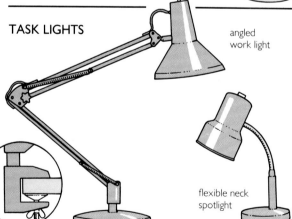

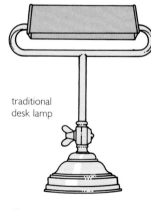

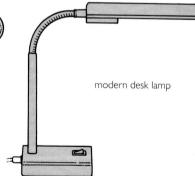

angled work light

flexible neck spotlight

traditional desk lamp

modern desk lamp

ANGLED WORK LAMP
Style The strong, angular lines are appropriate for workrooms and some modern styles but may not suit a traditional setting.
In use Versatile spring-loaded arms and swivel head are easily adjustable. Clipped or clamped to a suitable surface, it takes up little space so is ideal for cluttered areas. Also available with a heavy, stable base.

FLEXIBLE NECK SPOTLIGHT
Style A small neat lamp that is equally at home in the workshop, on a desk or as a bedside lamp.
In use The flexible stem can be adjusted to almost any angle and the lamp is small and light enough to move around easily. (A clip-on version is available.)
Watchpoint The area of illumination is limited by the small size of the lamp.

Designed to give localized areas of bright light for detailed work, they can also be used for background lighting if redirected to bounce light off walls or ceiling. For maximum flexibility choose adjustable lamps so that you can direct light exactly where you want it.

DESK LIGHT
Style Available in both traditional and modern designs.
In use Gives an efficient, even spread of light for desk work. Some shades can be angled to alter the area lit. Some modern styles take a miniature fluorescent bulb, which is cooler to work under.
Watchpoint The shade should be at eye level to avoid glare.

CEILING LIGHTS

A central pendant is not the only choice – look, too, at downlighters, strips, spots and tracks.

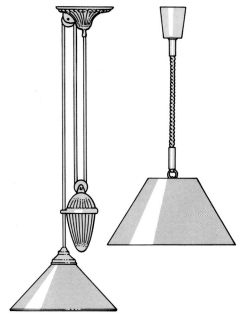

Most rooms have some sort of ceiling light, usually a single, central fixture, but the choice also includes fluorescent strip lights, downlights, spotlights and track systems. The light they give can be background, task or decorative, but unlike floor and table lamps, most ceiling lighting is permanent, with the wiring hidden in the walls or above the ceiling, so any change in position will involve some rewiring. It is important, therefore, to choose the right position the first time as it may be difficult to change without making a mess of your decorations or having the wiring exposed and visible.

PENDANT LIGHTS

The most common type hangs on a wire from the ceiling and gives background lighting or a more directional light, depending on the style of shade and the length of wire. If the fixture or shade is heavy, it will need additional support, usually a chain fixed into a joist.

A central pendant light can give a flat look to a room and cast ugly shadows. If you are redoing your lighting, consider installing a dimmer switch for the pendant to use with other lamps in the room or consider positioning it off center, low over a coffee table for example. Alternatively, an extended wire can be looped and fixed at another point on the ceiling.

Rise-and-fall fixtures

When fitted to pendant lights they become much more flexible. Positioned over tables or work surfaces, they can be pulled down or pushed up at will. There are two types of mechanisms available: one works on a pulley and balance, the other on a spring.

When rise-and-fall lights are lowered they can be uncomfortably bright, so choose shades carefully or use dimmer switches to control the intensity of the light. If this is not possible, use a low wattage bulb.

SHADES

Many of the shades shown for table and floor lamps are suitable for pendant lights, so you can match the shades in a room. A wide base opening distributes the light, while a narrow base opening concentrates the light downwards. Light from an open top shade reflects off the ceiling, adding to the general background lighting. The material the shade is made of makes a difference – opaque materials direct the light, while transparent materials diffuse it more evenly.

Decorative pendant shades

In addition to the fabric shades, there are pendant shades made from cane, paper, glass (plan, etched, stained and frosted), china, metal and PVC. Some metal frames have an inner reflective surface – to avoid glare use a crown silvered bulb.

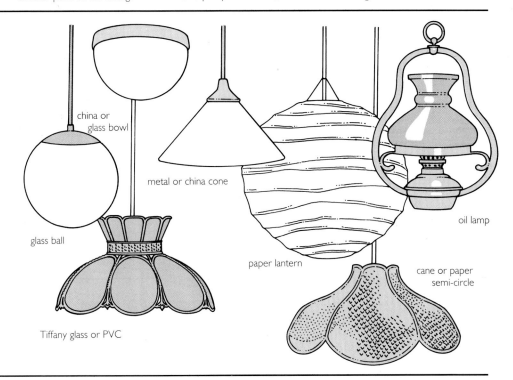

china or glass bowl

metal or china cone

glass ball

Tiffany glass or PVC

paper lantern

oil lamp

cane or paper semi-circle

CHANDELIERS AND LANTERNS

Style These range from the traditional crystal to the simpler branched metal or wood. Most are designed to take candles and bulbs and/or small shades. Reproduction Georgian lanterns have round or hexagonal sides.
In use Chandeliers suit rooms with high ceilings such as classically furnished halls, living and dining rooms. Lanterns should only be used in porches and halls.

Watchpoint The more elaborate the lighting, the more difficult it will be to clean. These heavy fixtures must have strong support. Suspend them from joists above the ceiling.

DOWNLIGHTERS

There are three types of downlights – recessed, eyeball and surface mounted – and each can have minor variations. Downlighters direct light away from the ceiling and make pools of light on horizontal surfaces and walls. Light is not reflected off the ceiling, so they are ideal for rooms with high or dark ceilings.

As the light is directional rather than diffuse, several downlights may need to be used. If they are wired to two different circuits and dimmer switches are used, a more flexible scheme is produced. To avoid glare the inner surface of the cylinder may be grooved to help direct the beam and reduce brightness when you look directly at the light.

RECESSED DOWNLIGHTERS

Style Attached flush to the ceiling with just the rim showing. Although modern in feel, these unobtrusive fixtures work in traditional rooms too.

recessed downlighter

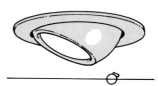

eyeball downlighter

surface-mounted downlighter

In use Most have fixed-position bulbs, which direct a broad beam of light downwards but some angled bulbs are available to spotlight a particular area. Wallwashers, which have up to half the opening covered, direct the beam over a wall where it is reflected back into the room.
Watchpoints A hole must be cut into the ceiling to fit the downlighter so once installed they are not easily moved. Check the depth between the ceiling and the floor above.

EYEBALL DOWNLIGHTERS

Style This semi-recessed spherical light is available in a white, silver or brass finish.
In use Can be swiveled to any position to highlight objects or reflect off the walls.
Watchpoint Slightly more obtrusive than the recessed downlighter. Can look out of place in traditional rooms.

SURFACE-MOUNTED DOWNLIGHTERS

Style The circular or square mounting is attached to the ceiling, no need to cut a hole in the plasterboard.
In use Suitable for high ceilings or those without sufficient space between ceiling and floorboards above for recessed downlighters.
Watchpoint More obtrusive than the recessed downlighter. There are fewer styles to choose from.

SPOTLIGHTS

Style Spotlights can be circular (eyeball), have a drum- or cone-shaped shade or a parabolic (controled beam) reflector. They can be ceiling mounted singly, in pairs or threes on a base; track mounted; or with a clip-on attachment.
In use They produce accent lighting to illuminate a work area, show off a decorative object or reflect light off a

wall or ceiling. Framing spots can be adjusted to light a specific area such as a picture.
Watchpoint They were particularly fashionable in the '70s and some models can look dated, so use with care.

TRACKS

Style Tracks for spots are usually ceiling mounted but they can be recessed, wall-

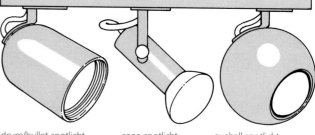

drum/bullet spotlight   cone spotlight   eyeball spotlight

triple spot fixture

parabolic spotlight

mounted or suspended from the ceiling. Lengths can be cut or clipped together for longer runs. Rigid L or T junctions or flexible connectors are available.

Mini tracks with small spots are much less obtrusive than the standard-size track. Single tracks work off one switch, multitracks work off two or more. Recently introduced tracks can take both tungsten and fluorescent bulbs so you can mix spots and strip lights.
In use The whole track carries the power so you can position

spots anywhere. The number of spots on any one track is limited by the wattage on the electrical circuit. Check with the shop when you buy. Position tracks parallel to walls or behind pelmets.
Watchpoints Tracks carrying spotlights are not advised for low ceilinged rooms. As the track is live do not use in bathrooms. Track systems are not usually interchangeable between manufacturers so you cannot choose a track from one manufacturer and lights from another.

STRIP LIGHTS

Style The bare strip light has been superseded by a range of attractively designed lights using warm fluorescent or tungsten bulbs, which give an even spread of light. The most basic fixture is the furring strip attachment, which is attached to the ceiling or the underside of a cabinet wall; the bulb is slipped between the ends.

Boxed fixtures with a grooved or etched glass shade gently diffuse the light and some come with safety features for use in bathrooms. Box shades, with

louvers set at right angles to the bulb, minimize glare when looking directly at the tube.
In use Ideal for concealed lighting under a run of kitchen wall cupboards, inside display cabinets, behind pelmets and bookshelves. A control box can be fitted to direct the beam.
Watchpoint Clip in furring strip fixtures can be unattractive so try to position them with the tube out of sight.

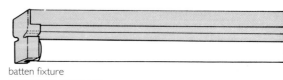

batten fixture

boxed fixture

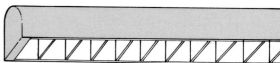

louvered fixture

WALL LIGHTS AND BULBS

Use wall lights for versatile background lighting, and choose the right bulb for every light fixture.

Wall lights are mainly used for general background lighting although some can also be used as task lights. Their position on the wall means they don't take up space but once they are attached, with the wiring chased into the wall, they are impossible to move without disturbing the entire area. It is important, therefore, that you are really sure where you want the lights so that they do the job required. Those for general background illumination will need to be high enough to bounce light off the ceiling; for reading, they should be lower.

The styles range from the traditional to the ultra-modern. Try to see them lit before buying, as the shades are usually positioned at eye level, making them particularly noticeable.

Wall lights are best wired to a separate circuit with dimmer switches giving a range of light intensity to suit every occasion. Some have an on/off switch on the fixture itself, others are controled from a wall switch.

There are four basic styles – bracket, bowl, bulkhead and strip – which are available in both modern and traditional designs.

Bulbs are described also to help you make the right choice of bulb for every fixture.

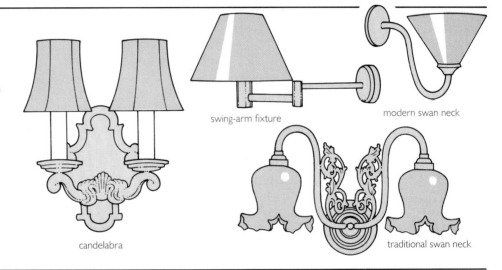

swing-arm fixture

modern swan neck

candelabra

traditional swan neck

BRACKET LIGHTS
Style Both single or double brackets are available. Traditional styles include the swan neck fixed with the shade facing up or down, single or double candelabra made in metal or wood, and more modern styles such as the swing-arm fixture.
In use Choose fixtures and shades that are in keeping with the decorative style of the room. Many shades that match those used on pendant lights and lamps are available.
Watchpoint If there is glare from the bulb when the shade faces down, try a crown silvered bulb.

SCONCES

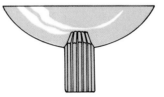

Style Made from plaster, ceramic, glass or metal, and attached flush to the wall, Designs range from half hemisphere, cone or fan to more decorative shapes. Choose plaster or ceramic for traditional rooms; chrome or glass for a modern setting.
In use Glass shades diffuse a soft warm light, while plaster and metal shades reflect light upwards. Some metal shades have an acrylic inset at the base, which reflects light downwards and against the shade. Plaster shades can be painted to match the wall.
Watchpoint For general lighting they must be positioned high on the wall so that light can be reflected off the ceiling.

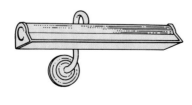
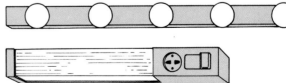

BULKHEAD
Style These functional lights have a high-tech utilitarian look.
In use Mainly used as task lights, so position them to cast light on the activity. Since the bulb is totally enclosed they are particularly suitable for bathrooms.

PICTURE LIGHTS
Style Usually made in brass with a swan-neck arm and swivel joint to angle the shade.
In use Can be attached to the wall or to the back of the picture. Use a double-ended tungsten strip bulb for best effect.

STRIP
Style Wall-mounted strip lights are usually found in bathrooms above mirrors. A modern variation is the row of small bulbs, mounted on a natural wood or metal strip, Hollywood dressing-room style.
In use The boxed shade fixture diffuses the light gently and may incorporate an outlet.
Watchpoint Buy one with a cord pull switch for safety in a bathroom.

BULBS

A change of bulb is an inexpensive way to transform the nighttime look of a room. The choice of bulb depends on four factors – color, cost of running, length of life, and, of course, the type of fixture in which it is to be used.

There are four main types used in the home: incandescent filament, tungsten halogen, low-voltage tungsten halogen and fluorescent bulbs.

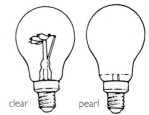

clear   pearl

INCANDESCENT FILAMENT BULB

The traditional light bulbs are known as incandescent bulbs. They screw into light fixtures.

The thickness of the tungsten filament determines the light's brightness, which is expressed as wattage: the most commonly available are 15, 25, 40, 60, 75, 100 and 150. Tungsten filament bulbs come in a range of sizes, shapes (including tubes for strip lights) and finishes.

Advantages Colors appear close to natural light, but with a warmer look.
Disadvantages Bulbs have a short life. They generate heat and cannot be used too close to paper or fabric shades.

Incandescent bulb varieties
Bulbs are made of clear glass, giving a crisp light, or pearl or white coated glass, giving a more diffused light. Colored bulbs are also available.
Shapes Apart from the traditional bulb there are:

☐ Large globe bulbs in clear or glare-free coated glass for decorative use without shades.
☐ Candle bulbs, either smooth or twisted, with a clear, pearl or white finish, for use in chandeliers, lanterns or wall lights – some have a flickering filament to look like an candle.
☐ Tubes, available in a clear or white coated finish.

Reflector bulbs
☐ Crown silvered bulbs reflect light back into any fixture that has a reflective surface; in turn, this reflects the light back into the room without dazzle.
☐ Internally silvered R bulbs have a frosted crown; the rest of the bulb is silvered and acts as a reflector. Designed to throw light in a beam – the shorter the filament, the narrower the beam of light. Use as an accent or task light at close quarters or in downlights

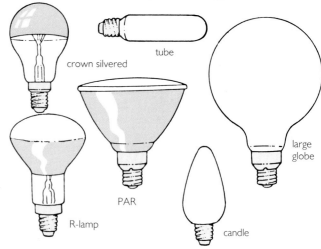

crown silvered   tube

R-lamp   PAR   candle   large globe

or wall washers for soft spotlighting. When buying, check that the lamp will take the bulb heat.
☐ Sealed beam units, known as PAR bulbs, consist of a glass lens sealed on to an aluminium-coated glass reflector. A clear lens gives a narrow beam; a faceted lens spreads the beam. Some bulbs reflect heat back into the fixture, which must be designed for these bulbs. Give considerably more light than the equivalent watt R bulbs. Use in downlighters or spots.

TUNGSTEN HALOGEN BULB

These bulbs produce brighter, sharper light than tungsten ones; they make colors look slightly less warm but blues look better. Watt for watt, they give more light. They need special fixtures and are used for spots and uplighters.
☐ Tiny bulbs with pin fixtures are used in portable lamps, downlights and track spots. They depend on a reflective shade to distribute beam.
☐ Linear bulbs give a broad beam and can be fitted into reflectors and downlighters.
☐ PAR tungsten halogen bulbs are also available.
Advantages Have twice the life of tungsten bulbs and are slightly less expensive to run.
Disadvantages The bulbs can get very hot so care must be taken with the light fixtures and their position. Don't touch the bulb – dirt or grease will crack it; handle with a clean cloth or paper sleeve. If touched accidentally, clean with mineral spirits.

LOW-VOLTAGE HALOGEN BULBS

They depend on faceted reflective shades to distribute the light – the smaller the facets, the narrower the beam.
Advantages The bulbs are small and compact and are good for discreet accent and display lighting. The filament is placed close to the reflector, which allows for precise positioning of the beam, ideal for spotlighting. The light produced is very crisp and concentrated so a lower wattage can be used. Longer life and cheaper running costs than tungsten bulbs. The heat is reflected back into the bulb making a cool beam.
Disadvantages They are expensive and need a transformer to convert electric current from mains to low voltage; never use them direct from a mains outlet. The wattage of the bulb must not exceed that of the transformer so get professional advice before buying. Some bulbs are very small and have a fragile pin fitting.

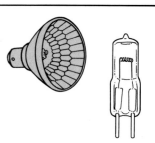

FLUORESCENT BULB

Originally gave colors a cool appearance. Warm ranges are available but colors still do not compare with tungsten. They give a diffuse background light. As well as the traditional long tube there are:
☐ compact doubled-back bulbs;
☐ single ended or PL bulbs used in desk lights;
☐ D-shaped or 2-D bulbs for task and decorative lights;
☐ ring-shaped bulbs.

You can replace a tungsten bulb with a compact fluorescent (SL) bulb with a screw fitting (25 watts is equivalent to a 100 watt tungsten bulb).
Advantages They have 4-5 times the life of a tungsten bulb, and are cooler and cheaper to run.

MINI FLUORESCENT BULBS
Give a flat white appearance to colors. Used in wall lights and concealed strip lighting behind pelmets, shelves, etc.
Advantages The bulbs are cool, good for desk and task lights, and economical to run.
Disadvantages Unlike the larger fluorescent bulbs, warmer color ranges have not been developed.

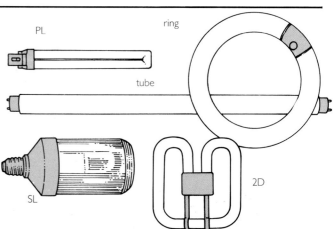

PL   ring   tube   2D   SL

FIREPLACE WALLS

A wall that contains a fireplace needs careful attention, whether or not you like to have open fires.

Traditionally, the hearth has always been regarded as the heart of the home. Particularly before the advent of radio and television, the family would gather around a glowing fire in the evenings to read, play games or talk.

For a while, though, it seemed as if the open fire was a threatened species as gas and electric fires, and later central heating, became increasingly common. Many fireplaces were blocked up, and elegant mantels discarded in favor of undoubtedly more efficient forms of heating.

Recent years have seen a revival of interest in the open fire. Although no longer regarded as a practical or efficient way of heating an entire house, the contrast between the comforting glow of flickering flames and bleak winter weather cannot be denied. Many families now lay a fire only in the living room, where its inviting warmth can be best appreciated by family and friends. And it is, of course, possible to retain a distinctive fireplace for its decorative value, to provide a handsome focal point for seating, even if it is not used.

The choices If you have a fireplace, think carefully before deciding how to deal with it, both in practical and decorative terms. You could replace the mantels, install a more modern heater or block it up and remove the mantel. A fireplace that has been covered over by a previous owner of the house can be re-opened without great difficulty, providing the chimney hasn't been blocked up. If you have no chimney at all, don't despair. A new flue, made from ceramic-lined metal sections, can be built up outside the house and clad in brick or built inside and concealed by a false chimney.

Decoratively, the fireplace itself must be viewed in relation to the chimney above and the side recesses. How these are treated affects the atmosphere of the entire room and plays an important role in highlighting or playing down the fireplace itself.

Around the fireplace
A fireplace wall begins with the fireplace, but it does not end there. The mantel, surrounding cabinets and custom lighting are equally as important to the look and feel of this living room.

DECORATING IDEAS

It goes without saying that the way you decorate the fireplace wall must blend in with the decor of the room as a whole. But because a fireplace wall has a structure of its own – generally with a protruding chimney breast flanked by recessed alcoves – it does require special attention.

Start by asking yourself how often you light a fire during cold weather – every day, on the weekends or only on rare · winter evenings? Your answer should influence the way you treat the fireplace wall. A frequently used fireplace should take pride of place in the room since it forms a natural focal point for warmth and interest; one that is infrequently lit should be allowed to merge into the background.

The fireplace If the existing fireplace is not to your liking, it should be easy to find one that suits your taste and budget and matches the style of your home. Antique, modern and reproduction versions are widely available.

Scale is important – a tall, imposing fireplace tends to overwhelm a small, low-ceilinged room, while a plain, modern fireplace can become lost in an imposing Victorian or Edwardian room.

Also bear in mind the fact that modern technical improvements can greatly increase the efficiency of the fire. And if you want the pleasure of real flames, without the bother of a real fire, consider a room heater (basically an open fire behind glass doors), or a gas or electric fuel-effect fire. In most cases a back boiler for heating radiators and hot water is optional.

The chimney breast and alcoves are almost always arranged symmetrically, so it's important to reflect this in the decoration. It is, for example, best to stand a pair of lamps on the mantelpiece or a standard lamp in each alcove rather than have a single, unbalanced lamp.

Traditionally, a large painting or mirror is centered above the fireplace, and both alcoves are treated identically. The alcoves should not fight for domi-

△ *Blue and white*
This elegant fireplace is painted white to match the intricate cove molding and picture rail. Thus the architectural detail of this period room emphasizes the lines of the chimney breast and alcoves, against a background of Wedgwood blue. A picture over the fireplace emphasizes the chimney breast and draws the eye away from the alcove.

nance with the chimney breast and fireplace. If the fire is often used, focus attention on the chimney, perhaps by using a different color or wallcovering than the one used in the alcoves.

If you light your fire less often, plenty of interest in the alcoves prevents the fireplace from dominating the room. Traditionally, built-in bookshelves or display shelves use the recess to best advantage, frequently with small cabinets at floor level. Another solution is to install modular storage or a small sofa in the space.

◁ **Old and new**
A period setting does not have to be furnished traditionally. In this alternative to the treatment below, an up-to-date tubular storage trolley in each alcove fits in well with both the fireplace and the cove molding.

▽ **Traditional elegance**
Symmetry is all important when decorating the fireplace wall. Here, a traditional approach has been taken – a large mirror tops the imposing fireplace and the alcoves have been arched over to frame glass display shelves. The arches and cabinets below are outlined in moldings of a similar style to that of the cornice.

MAKING CHANGES

If the fireplace has been removed entirely or blocked up, or it simply is never used, the wall to which it belongs needs a special approach.

An unused fireplace How you decorate such a fireplace depends largely on whether or not the mantel is attractive. If it is, decorate the entire fireplace wall as you would if the fireplace were in use. After all, no fireplace is used all year round, however bad the weather may be!

There are many ways of preventing the empty grate from becoming an eyesore. Traditionally, a fire screen was used. Other alternatives include a potted plant, an arrangement of dried flowers, leaves or even logs and fir cones. Whatever you choose, be sure that it is harmonious with both the mantel and the decoration above and next to it.

A blocked off fireplace It's always worth considering opening up such a fireplace – you never know what delights may have been hidden away behind a layer of boring Sheetrock. Opening up a fireplace should be done with care – it can be messy, and the condition of the firebricks, the chimney itself and the hearth must all be carefully checked if the fireplace is to be used again.

Treat a fireplace where the opening has been closed off (perhaps with a sheet of Sheetrock) but the mantel has been left in place, in much the same way as you would a fireplace that is not being used. It's often a good idea, though, to plan on using a fairly substantial display in order to hide a possibly unattractive covering.

If the mantel has been removed it's best to treat the entire wall – chimney breast and the alcoves – as a single entity in

△ *Modern simplicity*
In this home, two rooms have been combined into one – and the fireplaces in both have been removed. In one, the opening has been completely plastered over – in the other a perfectly square hole has been left. The result is an elegant sequence of angular recesses.

order to create a unified sense of space and to avoid the impression that something is missing. Try building cupboards or shelves out to the line of the chimney breast to hide all traces of the recessed alcoves.

Installing a fireplace in the absence of an existing chimney can be easier than you might think. Ready-made masonry chimneys, which can be installed either inside the house or on an outside wall, are now available, as are stainless-steel prefabricated chimney systems.

Using the chimney breast Where a fireplace has been removed, the redundant chimney breast often provides an excellent location for a central heating radiator.

The radiator could be unattractive in so prominent a position, and so an open latticework 'box' has been built around it. The lattice, which allows heat to radiate freely, is painted cream to tone in with the rest of the wall. The front of such a cover should be removable to allow access for repairs.

▽ *Supplementary heat*
Although central heating is a more practical and time-saving way of providing warmth, a real fire undoubtedly adds an inviting glow.

Here, one fireplace has been removed while the other (in the sitting area of the room) has been left in place, to be used in conjunction with the main form of heating. A modern mantel with simple lines blends well with the overall decor.

▷ **A bright effect**
The installation of arched windows on either side of the fireplace is a bright and unusual way to surround and highlight the fireplace wall.

Neutral-colored walls and a high ceiling with decorative white molding add to the elaborate but comfortable feel of this living area.

▽ **Sense of space**
A large mirrored fireplace wall gives this room added depth. Pale colors intensify the sense of space while decorative elements such as sleek modular furniture and vertical blinds enhance the modern feel.

FIREPLACES

The traditional fireplace is making a comeback and there's a shape and style to suit every home.

MATERIALS

The mantel and interior (infill or slips) of the fireplace can be made from a variety of both natural and man-made materials.

Ceramic tiles were popular as decoration on the interior (slips) of the fireplace in Victorian and Edwardian times. The tiles used were ornate and often decorated with flowers, fruit or leaves. Heavily embossed tiles in colors such as green, mulberry, brown and cream, or blue-and-white Delft designs, were also used. It was not until the 1920s that fireplaces were completely decorated with tiling, which could be plain, embossed, incised, or made to imitate stone, slate or marble. Tiled fireplaces are still made today. Tiles are easy to clean, but chip and crack if anything heavy is dropped on them.

Stone and slate Both are popular for 'rustic' style fireplaces. Stone comes in a variety of colors, including off-white, honey, gold and gray. Quartzite, which has bands of color running through the stone and a slight sparkle, is a popular choice. Stone can either be carved to the shape of the surround or pieced from regular or random-shaped blocks. The surface of these blocks can be textured (chip-like surface) or smooth. Slate ranges in color from blue-green to dark gray and black. Like stone, it can be polished or textured.

Metal has always been a popular material for fireplaces. The Victorians made elaborate cast-iron fireplaces. Today, copper, brass, wrought iron and stainless steel are used to make canopies, mantels, fire opening edging and other accessories.

Briquettes are made from reconstituted brick. They vary in size from actual house brick dimensions to much slimmer versions, half the thickness, and are available in a variety of colors. They are used to build fireplaces in all sorts of styles and are most common for DIY fireplace kits.

Marble has been a popular material for building fireplaces since the late 17th century. It comes in a range of colors, including white veined with gray or black, rose, green, brown and dark gray. Today reconstituted marble (lighter and cheaper than the real thing) is often used on the fireplace interior. Real marble is used to make expensive mantels and is used in sheet form on the fireplace interior.

Fibrous plaster can be molded to imitate classic designs formerly made from marble or carved stone, but is much lighter in weight and cheaper. It is usually accompanied by an interior of real or reconstituted marble. Plaster surrounds are available from specialist shops.

ANATOMY OF A FIREPLACE

Before buying a fireplace, it is useful to know the names of the various parts.

Mantel This can also be called the surround. It is the outermost framework around the fire, usually consisting of two vertical uprights and a horizontal plinth with a shelf on it – the shelf is known as the mantelshelf.

Fireplace opening This is the hole in the center where the fuel is housed. It is often edged with brass or other metal edging.

Interior, infill or slips The area – often marble or reconstituted marble – separating the fireplace opening from the surround.

Firebox, basket or firegrate These hold the burning fuel.

Hearth Strictly speaking this is the concrete or stone base upon which the fireplace is built.

Decorative hearth This is the slab on the floor that extends (by a minimum 12in.) in front.

Fireback Traditionally decorative cast iron, but can be made of stone, fire clay or firebricks. This is the backplate against which the burning fuel is housed. It protects the back of the chimney from the heat of the fire.

Wood Pine, oak, walnut and a variety of hardwoods are used to make mantels. When used for a classic style fireplace, the wood is combined with a marble, tiled, or cast iron and tiled interior. Modern and rustic styles usually have an interior of real stone or briquettes.

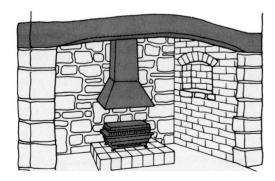

INGLENOOK

Style The traditional cottage fireplace – a big alcove that contains a fire, and sometimes seating. Modern inglenook designs are made from briquettes or stone.

In use The inglenook cannot be bought ready-made. It is either an original feature or can be custom-built. The fire itself is usually housed in a fire basket on a raised plinth and the smoke guided into the wide chimney via a brass canopy or hood. A freestanding or solid fuel appliance suits it well.

TUDOR

Style Large stone fireplace with a carved mantel and big, arched opening. The fuel is housed in a fire basket. In the summer when not in use, the fireplace opening can be filled with a traditional tapestry firescreen.

In use Strictly for big rooms, preferably those furnished in dark oak and with period features. Originally Tudor fireplaces could stand around 6½ft. high and 6½ft. or more wide. Nowadays, reproductions are available in more modest dimensions; typically around 56in.high×60in. wide.

CLASSIC
Style This has a carved mantel made from pine, fibrous plaster, white-painted hardwood or marble. The interior is usually made of real or reconstituted marble slabs and the fireplace opening edged with brass or stainless steel. Alternatively it can be made without an interior so a fire basket can stand in the wide opening.
In use Not suitable for small rooms with low ceilings as this fireplace typically stands around 49in. high and 70in. wide.

DRAFT-ASSISTED FIREBOX
You can now buy draft-assisted fireboxes that enable you to adjust the rate at which solid fuel burns. Basically, dampers (manually operated levers) or a small fan (electric operated) control the flow of air from the room into the fireplace. This makes burning efficient and helps to stop heat from disappearing up the flue. It also means the fire can be kept on all night by reducing the rate of burning to a smoulder. It looks just like an ordinary grate, but has dampers at the side or bottom. The fan-operated type blows air into the room.

TILED
Style Tiled fireplaces were popular from the 1920s onward with many post-war examples made in two-tone colored tiles. More recently these have been updated with more stylish and streamlined 'designer' styles.
In use The tiles of baked clay are easy to clean and maintain, but do have a tendency to chip or crack if heavy objects – a poker for example – are dropped on them. Sizes vary; modern examples are typically around 32in. high×49in. wide.

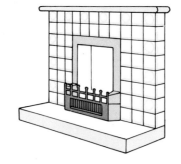

VICTORIAN
Style Can be either ornate cast iron with a wide arched or square opening and fire basket for the fuel or a carved wooden surround combined with ornate interior (infill) tiling and opening edged with cast iron, topped by a small canopy.
In use Sizes vary enormously from the large – around 60in. high×56in. wide – to those much smaller, originally intended for bedrooms. Those with a pine mantel are suitable for cottage-style interiors; bigger designs look best in large, period-style rooms.

RUSTIC
Style Various designs made in briquettes or stone, available in kit form or custom-built.
In use For small rooms, look at neat briquette fireplaces with arched openings, or the smaller stone fireplaces, which usually have a wooden mantel and shelves on each side of the surround. If you have the space, choose from a range of larger fireplaces. These consist of a low plinth topped by wood or stone, built into the alcoves at either side of the chimney breast. The chimney breast can also be stone clad.

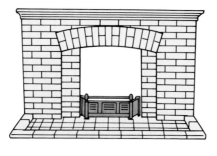
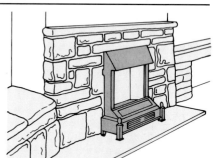

HOLE-IN-THE-WALL
Style As the name suggests, this is simply an opening in the wall or chimney breast, fitted with a basket to hold burning fuel. Many fireplace shops sell brass edging to fit around an old fireplace opening and turn it into a hole-in-the-wall fireplace. More elaborate hole-in-the-wall designs have a stone, slate, or brick plinth below the fireplace opening (as shown).
In use The opening must be a minimum of 16in. wide. Especially suitable for a modern house.

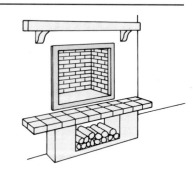

FIRE-IN-THE-MIDDLE
Style Modern, high-tech or rustic, depending on materials used. The fire, as the name implies, stands in the middle of the room. It comes in many styles; built into a chimney breast where the walls either side have been knocked through, as shown; alternatively, at a cost you can have a central chimney professionally built. Or the fire can be housed in a basket on a raised stone platform in the center of the room with a copper, wrought iron, or steel chimney, which starts as a wide canopy above the fire then narrows to a circular or square flue.
In use Often installed in large, open-plan rooms as a dividing line between one area and another. The room must be large for this sort of fireplace to look effective.

INDEX

PHOTOGRAPHIC CREDITS
Camera Press/Schoner Wohen, 12-13, 15, 16 (top)
Casa Viva, 36-37
Dulux, 40-41, 42, 44 (top), 89
Phillip H. Ennis Photography, 2-3, 4-5, 11, 22 (top), 35, 38 (top), 44 bottom
EWA/Guy Bouchet, 39
EWA/Michael Crockett, 91
EWA/Michael Dunne, 25, 32 (bottom), 38 (bottom)
EWA/Frank Herholdt, 78
EWA/Rodney Hyett, 65
EWA/Tom Leighton, 76-77
EWA/David Lloyd, 88
EWA/Spike Powell, 79 (top)
EWA/Jerry Tubby, 80 (bottom)
Faber Blinds Ltd, 37 (top)
Martyn Goddard, 90
Habitat, 6, 14, 45
Hulsta UK Ltd., 34 (top)
Jalag/Peter Adams, 43, 80 (top right)
Jalag/Zuhause, 18-19, 20, 21 (top), 29, 34 (bottom)
The London Door Company, 27 (bottom)
Melabee M. Miller, 17, 23, 28 (bottom), 44 (top), 79, 92 (bottom)
National Kitchen & Bath Association, 22
National Magazine Co/David Brittain, 46-47
National Magazine Co/John Cook, 16 (middle)
National Magazine Co/Good Housekeeping, 61
Pella/Rolscreen, 92 (top)

Perrings Home Furnishing, 20 (bottom)
The Picture Library, 26, 47 (bottom)
PWA International, 21 (bottom)
PWA/Living Magazine, 62, 63, 64
Quaker Maid, 30 (top and bottom)
Rutt, 37 (bottom)
Stag, 66 (bottom)
Sunway Blinds, 27 (top)
Syndication International, front cover, 1
Syndication International/Homes and Gardens, 16 (bottom), 75
Syndication International/Ideal Home, 24
Jerry Tubby/Eaglemoss, 80 (top left and bottom)
Ulrich Inc., 87

DESIGNER CREDITS
Steve Ackerman, 35
Caron Avery, 22 (top)
Beverly Ellsley, 11
James Ferreri, 4-5
Andrew James Iatridis, Architect, 28 (bottom)
Daniel Mullay Interior Design & Decoration, 79
Norma Pofsky, Interior Designs, 92
Katherine Stephens, 66
Susan Rosenthal, ISID, 17, 23, 44 (top)
Diane H. Small, CKD, 22
Sue Stevens and Debbi Seymour, 44 (bottom)
Sue Stevens, 2-3